MEANING MATTERS

ALENA BENNETT

Having worked with Alena, she is perfectly placed to share her wisdom and knowledge with us. Her energy and enthusiasm for growth is infectious and every woman in finance would be lucky to have Alena in their world. I would have loved to have had a book like this earlier to help me navigate my career in a more purposeful manner.

Nital Scott, Chief Financial Officer, Beautycounter

I have experienced personally the positive impact of Alena's work. I call her my secret weapon. She balances her creative flair with a very intelligent approach. Every woman in finance who wants to elevate their potential should have a copy of this book or experience Alena 1-1 as they will deeply benefit from it.

Stella Petrou Concha, Co-CEO Reo Group, Listed as Australia's Top Ten Women Entrepreneurs 2018, Global Goals Advocate

Having worked with Alena over the last 12 months as my coach, but also as my friend of over 15 years, I have personally experienced her passion in working with women in Finance as well as her ability to inspire her clients and friends to be their best selves and achieve their career goals. The fact that she has made her ethos and approach accessible to everyone by sharing her work in this book demonstrates her generosity and commitment to helping everyone achieve their best in their own meaningful way. It can be eye opening to come to realisations about yourself and your experiences in the workplace through reading this book but to understand that many women feel the same way is invaluable. Everyone should have a copy of this insightful, yet very practical book.

Emma Roche, General Manager, Group Finance and Investor Relations, Ruralco Holdings Limited

Alena is leading the path of inclusiveness, empowerment and equality. Her book gives you a clear and easy path to fast track your career to where you always dreamt it could be. It is a must for any woman in finance who feels she has more to give, but not sure 'how' to do it.

Rita Serna, Global Audit, Bechtel Corporation

Getting more representation of women in senior leadership roles is still such a challenge today. We need more women like Alena who have the context, experience and skills to guide women and organisations in making this possible. This book is a great resource for any woman looking to turn insight into action and thrive at work in a way that has greater meaning than just delivering results.

Marissa Gomes, VP Brand Marketing at Cobram Estate Olive Oil

Alena is a unique professional I'm privileged to have met. She is able to use her professional training and experience combined with her emotional intelligence and compassion for others to bring the best out in individuals and teams. In this current landscape of constant change, it's more important than ever to have highly engaged teams of people who genuinely understand they are valued. That's where Alena, and this book, can help! Alena has so much passion for her work, and Women in Finance are fortunate that this energy is directed at helping them. The practical tools in the book will help readers find purpose and create a meaningful career.

Alison Flemming FCA, General Manager Finance, Scentre Group

Finally, someone has written a book for women in finance! With her experience and skill, Alena is perfectly placed to show us how purpose directly leads to better, more meaningful outcomes at work. This book cleverly turns insight into action so that women in finance can make the change they want.

May Fuh CA, CPA, Director, Strategic Initiatives,
BMO Private Wealth, Bank of Montreal

Meaning Matters

Results Beyond the Numbers

alena bennett

Copyright © 2019 Alena Bennett

First published in 2019 by Hambone Publishing
Melbourne, Australia

All rights reserved, except as permitted under the *Australian Copyright Act 1968*. No part of this publication may be reproduced, distributed, or transmitted in any form or by any means, including photocopying, recording, or other electronic or mechanical methods, without the prior written permission of the publisher, except in the case of brief quotations embodied in critical reviews and certain other noncommercial uses permitted by copyright law.

This book uses case studies to enforce the meaning behind its relevant chapter. Names have been omitted or changed to protect privacy.

Every effort has been made to trace (and seek permission for the use of) the original source material used within this book. Where the attempt has been unsuccessful, the publisher would be pleased to hear from the author/publisher to rectify any omission.

Typesetting and design by Eggplant Communication
Editing by Mish Phillips and Stephanie Ayres

For information about this title, contact:
Alena Bennett
alena@alenabennett.com.au
www.alenabennett.com.au

ISBN 978-1-922357-01-4 (paperback)
ISBN 978-0-6482011-8-2 (ebook)

CONTENTS

About the author   *viii*
Acknowledgements   *xi*
How to use this book   *xii*
Introduction   *xiv*

Part 1: ASPIRATION   1
1. Light up your motivators   3
2. Remove your mask   17
3. Plan for purpose   26
   3.1 Meta activity 1: Connect to your purpose   33

Part 2: ATTRIBUTES   45
4. Own your impact   47
5. Establish your powerbase   56
6. Do what matters   69
   6.1 Meta activity 2: Integrate your purpose   79

Part 3: APPROACH   91
7. Present with confidence   93
8. Communicate for influence   103
9. Bring change to life   118
   9.1 Meta activity 3: Create mastery through purpose   128

Final words   *141*
A note to organisations   *147*
An Invitation to continue the conversation   *153*

ABOUT THE AUTHOR

Alena (pronounced like the guy's name 'Alan', but with an 'a' on the end) loves to help people make the connections they need to unleash their potential. She combines her finance and leadership experience to shine a light on and bring out the best in people.

Alena delivers keynotes on the power of purpose in delivering superior results, while also mentoring and accelerating leaders to amplify their impact. She facilitates workshops on the enabling role of communication in cohesion and performance. Obsessed with helping finance executives deliver outstanding results beyond the numbers, she connects brains to hearts: within themselves, within their teams, and within their organisations. She understands that technical expertise only gets you so far and relying on this at the expense of other competencies results in stagnation. Stagnation is the nemesis of growth and ultimately, fulfilment.

Originally from Sydney, she grew up travelling around the world as a Navy brat and has continued to incorporate that sense of mobility and adaptability into her work and life. Often described as a 'chameleon', she uses her awareness of self and others to adapt her communication and behaviour to consistently deliver success: whatever the situation or environment. Having started afresh many times, she also knows how to take the lead and be the creator of her own destiny.

A Chartered Accountant, she successfully completed her US CPA exams while working in San Francisco, and amongst leading audits of large SEC registrants, she managed to strengthen some stereotypical perceptions that Australians were all 'dinkie die' and had kangaroos as pets!

As someone used to being different because of her tricky name, her brown skin, height or crazy hair, Alena believes that embracing diversity is the #1 key to equality, both in the workplace and in society.

Her client base, whilst having a finance focus, models this diversity. She has worked with leaders and companies such as KPMG, EY, Scentre Group, First State, CPA, AIQS, icare, Ruralco Holdings, Reo Group, Latitude Financial, just to name a few.

Prior to running her leadership consultancy practice, Alena held senior leadership roles in Audit and Corporate Finance in Australia and the United States. She is a wife and mother of 2 gorgeous but cheeky girls, aged 6 and 7.

Her mission is to change the world by enabling everyone to have a voice, because in her words:

"When people have a voice, we gain access to the best ideas, actions and values to inspire the world.

When people have a voice, they speak in a way that others want to listen.

When everyone has a voice, we can speak as equals.

When we speak as equals we can achieve our best."

She is proof that when you connect with your purpose and develop a voice, results always extend beyond the numbers.

alenabennett.com.au

For Leilani, Mila, Amira, Olina, Vienna Rose and Éire.

May you continue to thrive in the world as your beautiful selves and may we do our best to create it for you.

ACKNOWLEDGEMENTS

Thank you to everyone who has made this book come to life. It may be true, everyone has a book in them, but there is a reason that not everyone writes it! Life is tough and a lot goes on, and without the support of many people this book may not have been possible. Huge love goes out to all of you.

To my mentors and coaches, past and present, I salute you. Thank you for believing in me (even when I didn't) and showing me how to make my work more accessible to and consumable for the people I wish to serve.

To my clients past and present, I thank you. I learn and grow through our time together equally as much as you do. It is a privilege to walk alongside you and achieve your goals, and in doing so, I have the opportunity to achieve my own. As I tell you, you are always in my world.

To my amazing support team of virtual assistants, editors and designers – thank you for taking my crazy ideas and turning them into something way better than I could ever dream of. You make things happen.

To you…reading this book. I know your time is precious and valuable, and so I thank you for sharing some of that with me. Thank you for opting into the possibility of growth and in doing so opening your minds up to the ideas and insights I have shared. May this book inspire you into action so you may approach work with meaning and deliver results that matter to you.

Finally, to my ultimate powerbase: Cody, Leilani and Mila. You are my meaning. You are what matters. This is all for you. I love you.

HOW TO USE THIS BOOK

This book is intended to be a blend of insight and action. You are the experts of your own individual contexts and so I see my role as sharing with you some ideas that may stimulate relevant thinking and action that will amplify your impact at work in a way that is meaningful for you.

The book is structured in 3 sections: these are the keys to delivering 'Results Beyond the Numbers'. You have a choice…you don't need to read it front to back, in order, but you will absolutely reap massive rewards if you do! Your mind will continue to open up in a way that allows it to be ready for the next piece of learning or information.

However, not everyone needs everything, so it's important to know that you can 'pick and mix'. Most women that approach me need one or more of the following 3 things:

- Fulfilment
- Capability to improve performance
- Confidence

At the top, we have fulfilment and we achieve this through Section 1: Aspiration, which is all about the road to finding your purpose. Now, although we might love to just 'be more confident', I say you can't teach confidence. It emerges through both mindset and capability work. So working backwards from confidence, I have included in the book the key capabilities I know that women in finance need in order to improve their performance and progress their careers. You will find those primarily in Section 2: Attributes and Section 3: Approach.

If you are crunched for time, however, and want to use this as a guidebook, that will also work. (I have purposely made it a size that will fit nicely in your handbag!) Each chapter is filled with the relevant context and complementary activity so they can effectively be read on a stand-alone basis.

At the beginning of each chapter, you'll see I have hand selected a quote that sets an intention for you. You will recognise and be familiar with most of the amazing women I have included. I want to take an opportunity to recognise my dear friend and constant source of inspiration Linda Buchan, author of 'Step by Step: Finding my way back to me', who I have quoted in Chapter 4: Own your impact. As a high performer, with high potential, Linda faced adversity greater than anyone should ever have to face. Her personal story is raw and motivating beyond belief. She is the embodiment of 'owning it'.

Each chapter is intended to solve a problem. This is done to allow you to identify when you may need to utilise the content in the chapter. To facilitate this, I have included relevant activities and reflection questions that will move you from insight to action and fast!

At the end of every section of the book, I have integrated the key learnings into a Meta Activity. These are the big ones designed to consolidate your learnings in a way that has massive impact, with lesser effort. Many of the activities refer to models, lists or tables – and so for your convenience, I have templates on my website for you to download and use so you don't need to recreate the wheel. That said, I love a pen and paper as much as anyone, so feel free to write it in your own notebook your own way. Again, you know best what works for you.

Fundamentally, this book is about doing something for you. That has meaning to you. So that you can *be* you.

INTRODUCTION

The funny thing about working with numbers is that it's easy to start to feel like one. They're all you ever seem to talk about – and rarely in a positive context! The numbers don't reconcile, someone doesn't like the result this month, expenses are too high.

When you're fielding endless questions about the numbers, but no one ever stops to ask about *you*, it's probably no surprise that you start to feel replaceable. Of course, that feeling is only magnified when you're asked to work all weekend just because the system isn't churning out the 'right' numbers. (And when I say asked, I mean yelled at!) It gets worse again when you walk down the hallway and meet someone's eye with a smile, only to have them avert their eyes and quicken their pace. Where's the respect? The human decency?

Being treated as a number makes you feel undervalued, especially in a technology-forward world where apparently 'the robots are coming to take our jobs!' It's only natural that you would feel insecure and disposable. As if the fact that you have been there for years and that you have so much more to give counts for nothing. ('Counts' being the operative word!)

I appreciate how hard scheduling can be, but when I worked in a corporate environment, I remember feeling like the scheduling tool, Retain, was basically a poorly masked version of Tetris. The aim was just to fill as many rows as possible. Most of the time it was less a question of *who* you were filling the rows with, and more a question of simply filling them at any cost.

Picture a workplace where you're sat around a table, having a discussion about the most effective way to allocate people to tasks based on their interest and expertise. Where diversity of thought is perceived and acted on as a resource to be optimised, not as a fire to be put out. When you *let* the robots take the repetitive tasks so you can get on with the work that actually creates value! When you are confident enough in your ability and your sense of belonging to work up the courage to initiate this conversation. Work through the concepts and activities in this book, and that's exactly what you'll have.

How often do you walk into the office with gusto, excited about what the day will hold? If you answered, 'Not often', you're not alone. Women in finance often feel a bit 'meh' about their work. There's a feeling in our stomach telling us things just aren't quite right… but we're not really sure why. As that seemingly groundless dissatisfaction intensifies, we start to wonder, 'Is it just me? I'm in a pretty senior role, I'm capable at my job, I get paid well, and I no longer need to prove myself.' Spoiler alert: It's not just you, and none of these factors will give you the satisfaction you seek. Job satisfaction isn't about seniority, salary, and comfort. It's about pushing yourself, taking opportunities, and feeling like you're contributing in a meaningful way.

One of the biggest challenges women in finance face is the lack of female role models. Although women represent almost half of the financial services industry in some countries, in 2018 only 12.2%[1] of CFO positions were held by women globally. Similarly, we see that only 15%[2] of lead engagement partners auditing S&P 500 companies are women and only 24%[3] of investment managers are women, despite 55% of the financial services and insurance industry being females. However, a recent CEW (Chief Executive Women) report did show a small positive shift in the proportion of women in CFO roles in Australia, from 12%[4] in 2018 to 16% this year in their reported results.

The lack of female role models makes it really hard for women in finance to know what's expected and, more importantly, what's possible. To get the most out of our work, we need people we can aspire to emulate. People who demonstrate the behaviours or characteristics we believe will help us succeed. And we need at least some of those people to be women. How else can we learn how to achieve a senior position as a woman, how to have children without compromising on career, or how to stand up to sexism and gender bias in the workplace? How else will we know that it's even *possible* to do these things in our organisations?

When we can visualise what is possible for us in senior leadership, we step up and onto the path for progression. We work with the clarity and confidence to know that what we're doing is valued and valuable. We are treated differently by our peers, our staff and our leaders. Our effort to impact ratio improves: we have greater impact at work, and it even feels like it comes easier. The 'ambition gap[5]' closes and, woman by woman, the gender scales start to balance on an overall basis. When we know what we need to succeed, we can more readily do so. Follow the ideas shared throughout this book, and you will have what you need.

Gender diversity is now an imperative for ASX-listed entities. Most companies have now introduced some form of diversity and inclusion policy. And it's beginning to make a difference. As financial performance increases with gender diversity, companies see more clearly the benefit of gender diversity and become more proactive in their policies and practices. Wouldn't it be great to see the financial services industry research performed by McKinsey[6], showing the correlation between gender diversity and profitability and value creation, come to life in your organisation? The statistics showed those companies in the top quartile for gender diversity in their executive teams were almost 25% more likely to have above average EBIT performance than those in the bottom quartile. Not only that, a penalty existed for those companies that were low on gender diversity: they were 29% more likely to underperform on profitability.

With flexibility and parental responsibilities commonly sitting at the top of the list of barriers to finance leadership for women, consider this: if all the women in our organisation go on maternity leave only to come back, struggle to reintegrate, and eventually leave, that becomes our blueprint for the career path of women in our organisation. We may decide that 'this place isn't for me' and – to quote Sheryl Sandberg from her book *Lean In* – 'leave before we leave'. Not planning on reproducing? The grass isn't necessarily greener on the other side. You might easily be judged as 'less than' for not exercising your maternal 'duties'. Even if we manage to make it through our childbearing years unscathed, soon enough we'll be at the mercy of menopause. We'll cope in silence, of course, lest we be judged for hormones we can't control! I do wonder, if there was more gender equality in senior finance leadership, would expectations change? Would we still work these ridiculous hours? Or would someone have the courage to finally say enough's enough?

For the most part, women self-select out of the industry because 'life is hard enough already!' At the mid-senior level of leadership, there are precious few women left. There are so many fabulous women in finance who never reach their potential simply because they never get a chance to see what it could be. At some point in their careers they're going to look for someone to help guide them, to show them what's possible. And, like so many women before them, they're going to come up empty.

The four-stage journey

When you're a woman in finance, you generally go through a four-stage journey.

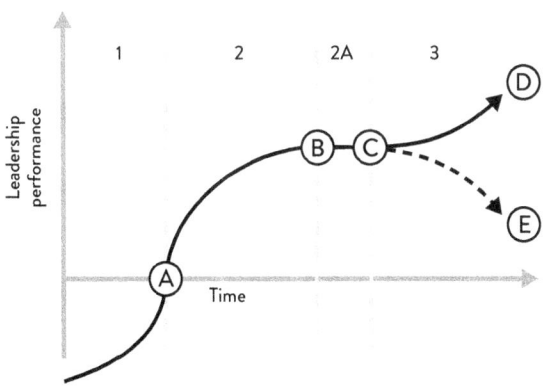

Stage 1 is the early stage of your career, where you are focused on learning. Learning the technical aspects, learning the industry, and learning what it means to exist in the corporate world.

Point A is where you move into your first leadership role, whether that be leading a team or managing other people. You are now in stage 2, and growth becomes the priority. As challenging as this stage can be, it is also very rewarding. Your performance and leadership capabilities improve exponentially, until ultimately your career trajectory reaches point B, a well-paid senior leadership position with clear requirements that you know how to meet. Life is good…

… until you start to feel the effects of stage 2A. This is where the growth stops, and you may start to feel like you're stagnating. You're not learning anymore, and your work isn't being valued. You know you have more to give, but there's no opportunity to give it. This is the point where work can really begin to feel like a hamster wheel.

Stage 2A can last any length of time, often continuing for years. As you get more and more bored, your performance starts to suffer as the sense of monotony and mindlessness prevents you from putting in your full effort. Gradually, over a long period of time, you begin to recognise that you've stagnated, and that the stress you're feeling isn't because of the work itself, but because you don't feel valued, or your work feels meaningless. You wonder how you are possibly going to get through the days. When you finally do reach that realisation, it can lead you down one of two paths.

Many women take this as their cue to simply quit (trajectory E). But to react in this way is to throw the baby out with the bathwater. As you'll learn in this book, this won't solve your problem, because you haven't yet done the work to truly understand what your problem is. You will move on to your next job with the root cause of your problem still very much intact.

The alternative is to start to move towards point D. And that's what this book is all about – helping you do just that. And I don't just mean if you're in stage 2A. Even if you're still in stage 2, you can use this book to move directly from B to D: from growing to thriving, *without* stagnating. The key lies in identifying your *aspiration*: what you care about and where you want to go. From there, you can develop the *attributes* you need to get to there, and follow a proven *approach* to regain your confidence and arrive at point D feeling strong and worthy. I want women in finance to thrive, and this book will show you exactly how.

In order to thrive, we need to focus on three key areas. These form the basis of the three parts in this book.

Part 1: Aspiration

This is all about identifying your aspirations – *where* you want to go. I find that women in finance often struggle to think big, or even beyond their immediate line of sight. This is particularly true of women in stage 2A, who are too busy battling their demons to see beyond them. Many women lack confidence, or make false assumptions that further limit the possibilities they see for themselves. But not you! Not anymore. This part is the springboard for you to deliver results beyond the numbers. This is where we get rid of that knot of dissatisfaction in the pit of your stomach and replace it with fire and excitement.

Part 2: Attributes

Part 2 covers the key capabilities and principles you need to set yourself up to achieve your aspiration. When you are clear on your vision, you will be able to clearly identify the key skills, attributes, and capabilites you need in your leadership toolbelt in order to get there. And with your newfound sense of meaning, you'll have the motivation to acquire them.

Part 3: Approach

Part 3 is about bringing your aspirations and attributes to life in a way that creates the change you need in order to get to point D. Essentially, it's about communciation – the capability that brings it all together! The words you say, the words you don't, your body language, your timing... and everything that goes along with it. This is one of the key capabilities you will need to continuously improve over time as you gain in seniority. It's about having the right conversations to build your attributes and reach your aspirations – without having to quit your job! It's about empowering yourself to change your problems into solutions.

One of my favourite movies is *Moana*. This gorgeous film follows the story of Moana, a young girl who is set to become Queen of the picturesque island of Motonui, where culture and community run deep. She dutifully observes how her father rules the island, training so that one day the island can be hers. Life is good! But before long, she begins to feel inextricably drawn to the water. What she thought were just beautiful childhood memories, she realises, is actually 'a calling'. So starts the friction between the good life she could live as Queen, and the great life she could create for herself by following this calling. Why am I telling you this story? Because I think this is exactly the challenge many women in finance face. Let me show you what I mean by sharing a story of my own.

I kind of fell into the world of finance. At the ripe old age of 17 I decided a commerce degree was the way to go. It was broad, and it would give me a good grounding in business. At the time I actually really wanted to work in physiotherapy, but I decided commerce was probably a safer bet 'for now'. At the time, Sydney Uni was the place to be, so off I went. In my penultimate year, when I got wind that people were starting to apply for work with the Big 4, I quickly jumped on the bandwagon. In the interview process, a female hiring partner told me, 'I work with amazing clients, who I end up actually being friends with, and I really help them!' Great relationships *and* helping people? I was sold. Little did I know that this was the beginning of my career as a bean counter!

Once the realisation hits you that there's a disconnect between what you love to do and what you actually do, there's no going back. It's not long before you convince yourself that you don't fit in, and from there the evidence-gathering machine that is your brain provides you with more and more 'proof' that this is indeed the case. Even if you recognise this as confirmation bias, it's too late, because you've already lost touch with an alternative. After so many years working in the same role, for the same male leaders, around the same male peers, you wonder whether you'd even be of any value elsewhere. Besides, your confidence is so far eroded that you probably couldn't articulate that value. You're so focused on the despair you feel in your current role that you can no longer remember all the awesome things you're capable of. You've lost *you*.

Sadly, this narrative is far from unique. And I think this loss of confidence is the biggest factor that drives women in finance to quit their jobs. When you are confident, your eyes and ears are open to the world, to feedback, and, most importantly, to learning. Because you are certain of your abilities, you own them, and you lean in to conversations or situations that allow you to demonstrate those abilities. You really 'show up' as the best version of yourself. But when you lack confidence in yourself, you shy away from opportunity. You hide. You make assumptions and generalisations about yourself that have little to no basis in reality. You extrapolate minor concerns into massive issues for yourself.

Self-defeating as it may be, this is normal! According to David Rock, founder and CEO of the NeuroLeadership Institute, certainty – the 'need for clarity and the ability to make accurate predictions about the future'[7] – is one of the five core domains of experience that trigger the threat-or-reward system in the brain. When certainty is removed, it triggers the brain's threat response and makes us want to run.

When women in finance lack confidence and certainty, they second-guess themselves. They interpret negative reactions to their ideas and conversations as a reflection of themselves and their own capability – their own worth. It might seem crazy to be bringing this up so early in the book, but it's an important part of the context.

Notwithstanding the upfront challenges of attracting women to the industry, graduate intakes often see pretty even numbers of men and women walking through the door. But look around you now – how many female peers do you have? What proportion of your leadership team are women? How many female execs are there in your organisation?

This context is the reality. Finance is a male-dominated environment.

Most women in finance start their career as a keen bean (counter, in my case!) and spend several years learning the detailed ins and outs of debits and credits, add-checking financial statements, getting coffee for the managers and partners, and fixing paper jams in the photocopy machine. From technical accounting and regulatory standards and industry knowledge through to discipline, perseverance, resilience, accuracy, and integrity, we're information sponges. And we're happy being sponges, because we can clearly see how these foundational skills and attributes will help us establish ourselves as businesswomen and provide us with job security over time. And that reiterates to us that the decision to pursue a career in finance was a good one.

As time goes on, we get promoted, undertake postgraduate study, and revel in the 'work hard, play hard' attitude. We're happy to be part of the crew and to be gaining valuable skills. So we go through the cycle of working Monday to Friday, studying weekends, and barely finding time for family and friends in between. We keep this up for years on end. And we do it all with a smile, because we know we're growing and improving.

In fact, this period is all about growth. Over these first few years we start to take on little leadership roles, whether that's leading a small audit team out on the field or a team of accountants, associates, or analysts. Very quickly, the teams get bigger and your responsibilities become greater. This is all on-the-job training for critical leadership skills – project management, team leadership, client service, stakeholder management – and you get that. You enjoy being the one staff go to for help, the one clients come to with questions.

The growth phase lasts a long time, because there are changes to so many aspects of your career – and life. Over my 15 years at KPMG, I had five or six different roles – not to mention two daughters! During that time, I accepted what turned out to be a really successful secondment to the San Francisco office. Over four years I was made manager and then senior manager, passed my US CPA exams, and met my now-husband. When I returned to the Sydney office, I took on a different role, moving into the technical advisory side of the organisation. But when it came down to it, I still was going with the flow. And that simply wasn't enough for me anymore. Anyone who has returned to the workforce after maternity leave will know that work as you knew it ceases to exist. The way you look at your work changes, and you begin to redefine your role. Yes, I had a nice office and a nice title, I worked with great people, and I was bringing home a good pay cheque. But I wasn't making any strategic decisions about my career.

It wasn't until I left KPMG and moved into my Head of Finance role at TAL – a financial services organisation - that my passion for people really crystallised. TAL was going through some impressive changes, and I knew from the training and change management work I'd done at KPMG that most people didn't like change! So I plucked up the courage to say to my new boss, 'I'd love to do this, but in order for me to implement improvements that are effective and sustainable, you need to have the culture in place to support it.' It was the first time I had been explicit about my love of working with and through people to achieve great outcomes.

I was starting to find my purpose.

I progressed rapidly during my time at TAL. I started a Finance Change Champion group; established a new, cross-functional leadership team; reinvented the year-end financial reporting process; and led the establishment of a new leadership team and function following a restructure. I was doing what I loved: connecting people, process, and performance; and provoking meaningful conversations across the finance function. Life was good. Little did I know that everything was about to change again.

I was participating in a leadership strategy day, watching the facilitator work his magic, when I had an almost childlike moment of realisation: *This is what I want to do when I grow up!* Everything I had been doing and feeling suddenly made sense. I had a passion for leadership and teams. There was only one issue: my day job was finance! I started to get that feeling. That feeling where things just don't seem right. Where you start to question why things are as they are. Where you start to have really strong opinions about how things should be done. This is what I call your tipping point.

In theory, you're on a great wicket right now. You've worked hard through the learning and growing phases, you're starting to really learn about your leadership style, and you're keen to create positive change within your organisation and for your team. But because you feel so unsettled, you don't act on this. Instead, you start to doubt yourself, your place in the organisation, and, sadly, your worth.

I call this a 'crisis of purpose'.

From here, if you can quickly identify your purpose, and it aligns with the work you're already doing, you become unstoppable. You get to Point D on the journey map, and fast! Like getting on the freeway and moving the gearstick into fifth, you move straight from growing to thriving. And it feels great! When your work is aligned to your purpose, it's no longer just about dollars and cents, trends, budgets and forecasts. Everything you're doing is for a reason – a reason you believe in at your very core. Knowing *why* you're doing the work makes you better at your job and allows you to contribute more fully and holistically. And it also makes you more resilient, because being invested in the end game makes the long nights, the difficult conversations, and even the fifth re-write of that presentation all worth it.

But as we know, not all women live out this story. If you reach that tipping point and you can't answer the *why*, your inner critic is activated. That little voice starts to whisper, 'Is this worth it? Why are you doing this? What you do doesn't matter. It's just a job.' All the confidence you've built up through years of opportunity, experience, and success starts to erode away. Over time, this starts to impact on your performance. You start on the downward trajectory to E. Now you start to think that you're not good enough, that this job just isn't for you. How, you wonder, have you not seen this massive misalignment until now?

Meaning: The missing ingredient

To really succeed in finance, you *need* to identify your purpose. And not just identify it, but know how to execute on it – not in some other job, not at some arbitrary point in the future, but exactly where you're at. Let me be clear: I don't mean to imply that this is going to be easy. (I remember being told once, 'You just need to go and find your passion, then everything will be okay'. Ah… not helpful!) Finding your purpose is a difficult process, fraught with emotion. It's also the only way to find the success and satisfaction you seek.

When a woman in finance is shown the path to discover her purpose and the meaning behind what she does, she becomes unstoppable. She becomes unstoppable because of the emotions she feels when she writes her purpose on paper. She becomes unstoppable because of the conviction that stirs in her stomach as she reads those words aloud. And she becomes unstoppable because of the commitment she makes to herself as the tears begin to well in her eyes. I see this time and time again in my clients. This is my wish for you.

To achieve your goals and find purpose in what you do, so that you can deliver results that mean far more than just the numbers, we need to address three core things:

1. Your cause: your purpose, your vision, your mission
2. Your capability: what you know how to do, and what you need to learn how to do
3. Your confidence: what makes you shine

Through this book, we will address each element in turn, with each one forming a necessary foundation for the next. As you work through this book, and have ping after ping of 'a-ha!' moments, you'll find that you feel stronger, deliver better, and progress faster, because you finally 'get it'. Like a baby finally realising it's her own reflection staring back at her from the mirror, you'll see yourself in a whole new way. And what you see will be awesome!

The strategies in this book will open you up to using 100% of your potential capability and elevating yourself above the pure technical skills that to this day are still the primary focus for many finance leaders. In a data-rich world run by bots, it's not technical knowledge that will get you places. It's all that other stuff! I appreciate that this is a challenging mindset to overcome – it's not easy to shake such deeply ingrained ideas. But when you can look beyond the numbers and facts to do 'soft skills hard', you embrace whole-brain thinking, and you open up an endless toolbox for sustained success.

This longer-term, more strategic approach will see you consistently raising the bar. If you do the work I lay out for you, I promise you will hit all your numbers, KPIs, performance benchmarks, bonuses and promotions. But, more importantly, you will deliver results beyond the numbers – developing people, improving processes, and lifting organisational potential. The impact of this change in mindset is huge.

When you make meaning matter, you can access the internal strength and resilience to push through those tough moments when you just want to throw your computer out the window. You can access perspectives that will service you and help you creatively solve problems. You can last the distance and be confident in the face of adversity, because you know it's for a reason you believe in.

All that remains now is for you to find that reason.

I have made this book as practical as possible so you can take immediate action and make immediate gains. Because I believe in the intent of the following well-known exchange:

CFO: 'What if we invest in developing our people and they leave us?'
CEO: 'What if we don't and they stay?'

In case you're wondering what happens to Moana, she leaves Motonui expressly against her father's wishes and goes out on her adventure so she can restore the heart of Tefiti. Because in her mind and soul she knows that this is what she was born to do.

It's time to find *your* purpose.

PART 1:
ASPIRATION

1 LIGHT UP YOUR MOTIVATORS

> "When you have a strong enough 'why', the 'how' will appear – it's like that sudden clarity when you de-mist your windscreen."
>
> Kerri Pottharst

One of the things I've really struggled with in my leadership consultancy practice is that much of the IP and content creation process is done alone. As someone who is energised by working with people, spending even two consecutive days alone can feel like torture. I'm at my best when I'm surrounded by people, which is why I choose to partner with organisations and individuals who share the same values as me and who are keen to invest in hands-on work on a longer-term basis. If I'm on my own for too long, my productivity goes down, my mojo goes down, and no doubt the quality of my work eventually goes with it.

Lack of motivation can become a vicious downward spiral. When we aren't motivated, everything feels like a grind. Our performance goes down. And when we let that attitude permeate our work, our decision-making ability becomes impaired. For example, if you're knee-deep in a spreadsheet and you hate getting into that level of detail, you might unknowingly shortcut the detailed analysis process by making an incorrect assumption. In so doing, you risk coming to the wrong conclusion simply so you can get out of the weeds.

The link between motivation and performance

Working in ways that don't align with our motivators jeopardises all-important accuracy, makes us less efficient, closes our minds to good ideas and solutions, and therefore reduces our overall effectiveness. Not only that, but when we are constantly working in conditions that are fundamentally at odds with our work preferences, we often catastrophise and waste time analysing scenarios that may never even come to pass. You might know this as 'entropy'.

When we don't know our motivators, we lack the basic information we need to be successful. Of course you feel dissatisfied if you've never even taken the time to identify what *would* satisfy you! Until you know what truly motivates you within your core, you don't know what will fulfil you. Do you sometimes find yourself feeling like you're banging your head against the wall? Or wondering why seemingly simple tasks feel so painfully difficult? How many times have you felt yourself slipping down this path? These are signs that you're out of touch with your motivators.

But what is it that gives us our motivation? How can we first understand, and then intentionally foster it? This chapter is your opportunity to find out.

When you know your motivators, you can align your tasks, resources, and working conditions with them. By doing this, you reduce the base level of friction in your workday. It's similar to removing the non-value-added steps from a process, or sending a different person to a meeting because their skill set better matches the task. By working in line with your motivators, you accelerate the process of reaching your ideal outcome.

What do you think of when you hear the word 'motivation'? Maybe you jump straight to the "ra-ra, we've got this" kind of motivation, or the motivational quotes on your Instagram feed that give you a pep in your step for all of about five minutes before fading from memory. That's not what I'm talking about here. For me, motivation is about implementing action-oriented, results-based preferences at work so that you can work faster and smarter. It's about having the awareness to take a step back, stop waiting for motivation to magically happen, and actively approach your work in a way that inspires you and makes you feel good.

In his book *Drive*[8], Daniel Pink explores the notions of extrinsic and intrinsic motivation, taking us through the evolution of humanity and the forces that drive our behaviour. Back in prehistoric times, we were motivated primarily by our need to find resources to survive. Pink calls this 'Motivation 1.0'. Over time, and with the Industrial Revolution, 'Motivation 2.0' emerged, which is all about the 'carrot or stick'. That is, we began to be motivated not only to survive but also to either obtain a reward (carrot), or escape a threat or punishment (stick). The idea is that we will repeat behaviours that result in a reward, and stop behaviours that are associated with a punishment. Most companies are aware of this type of motivation, and have some sort of EBITDA or UPAT target that drives the 'corporate bonus' element of employees' remuneration. By giving everyone some 'skin in the game', they motivate their employees to achieve better results for the company. Motivations 1.0 and 2.0 are both extrinsic, meaning they are reliant on factors outside of ourselves.

Pink then moves on to Motivation 3.0: *intrinsic* motivation. He asserts that people are motivated to do things to achieve a feeling of fulfilment within themselves, regardless of any potential reward. We see this every day. Women in finance often have a deep need to help people, not because they expect to get anything from providing that assistance, but because it feels inherently rewarding. This is at the core of intrinsic motivation. Now consider the decision to learn a new language at a mature age. For most people, this choice would have nothing to do with their job, and everything to do with a love of learning new things, or a desire to connect with a different culture. In my spare time, I teach ladies to run. These ladies don't do it to win a race or to receive anything in exchange for learning to run. They do it because it's fun, and it makes them feel good.

The distinction between intrinsic and extrinsic motivation is critically important in the fast-paced world of finance. Finance is deeply results focused – it's literally all about extrinsic rewards. We're focused on delivering outcomes – and rightly so! Without outcomes, the company would cease to exist. But to focus on this at the exclusion of all else is dangerous. Instead of considering what drives people to do their best, many companies allow politics and corporate scapegoating to creep into the workplace. Colleagues are thrown under the bus for individual gain. Work becomes compartmentalised and inefficient. And the culture becomes toxic. Ultimately, it's the most valuable, hard-working employees that resign.

So what's the answer? We need a balance between the two styles of motivation.

The challenge for women in finance is: How do we bring intrinsic forms of motivation into such a results-driven world?

Think about what drives you to willingly work those late nights at year-end, or when a transaction is about to close, or when your team needs a bit of extra support. Yes, there's a deadline you need to meet. And maybe you'll get some sort of recognition for the extra hours. But at the heart of it, that's not what makes you stay. It's about being there for your team and your boss. It's about sticking around because you fundamentally believe that you are the right person to help out. It's about knowing you've done your best and delivered to your values. *That's* what keeps you there. I've got to say, I will never forget the insanely late nights I pulled for one particular audit client. It was ridiculous! I would pull repeated all-nighters, only leaving my desk at 6 am when the manager finally walked in the door to start her shift. It was pure self-determination that kept me going.

In contrast, it's those late nights where you start to feel resentful towards your work, your boss, and possibly even your team that show you've fallen out of sync with your intrinsic motivation. It's actually got nothing to do with your boss or your team – it's nothing personal. It's not even the relative lateness of the nights. It's that you've lost that sense of control – you've stopped doing it for *your* reasons. When you're not working in alignment with your intrinsic motivators, the impact on your efficiency, effectiveness, and fulfilment is tangible.

The type of motivation that we can best control, and that allows us to very quickly increase our impact at work, is intrinsic. Why? Because it exists entirely within ourselves, and doesn't rely on any external factors. It revs you up and gets you going because it's meaningful to you as a person.

The thing about intrinsic motivators is that they happen at a *subconscious* level. It takes purposeful intervention to bring them to a conscious level. But once we do that – once we make the intangible tangible, and the implicit explicit – we have more knowledge at our disposal. And we can apply that knowledge not only to our own situation, but to those around us as well. When we take actions based on conscious awareness of what motivates us, the return on investment is immediate and visible. Imagine how your team's output would change if you set everyone up to work in ways that aligned with their motivators. All of a sudden, everyone would be working in fifth gear – not just for longer hours, but at their most efficient and effective. Performance would skyrocket, and your team would be happy!

I do a lot of work using the Inventory of Work Attitudes and Motivators (iWAM) tool. iWAM measures 48 'metaprograms' in your brain, which all operate at the subconscious level. Up to 60% of our behaviour at work is driven by these subconscious patterns, and yet they occur mostly outside of our conscious awareness. It's a bit of a daunting thought, I know! These 'motivating patterns' show which parts of your work, and which ways of working, are most interesting to you.

What I find particularly useful about iWAM is that it is highly detailed, but the language is simple and the information practical. iWAM scores you low or high for a particular pattern depending on how well it aligns with your personal preferences. For example, if you prefer to work in groups, your 'Group environment' pattern is high. If you prefer to pull together a plan before you start a new activity, your 'Structure' pattern is high.

When you are working in an environment that is aligned with your higher motivating patterns, everything feels easy, enjoyable, and efficient. You're putting in less effort but making more progress. It's a bit like driving on a freeway in fifth gear. You're doing 110 km/hr, but it couldn't feel smoother and the fuel meter is barely even budging. On the other hand, when you're working in an environment that is not aligned with your high patterns, you're more likely to feel a lot of friction at work – like you're pushing the accelerator but someone's got their foot on the brake.

Let's look at a few of the iWAM patterns that are most relevant to women in finance. This is only a handful of the patterns iWAM assesses, but they are a great starting point for you to start to visualise what your motivators might be in these areas.

Environment

Whether we prefer to work in a group or individual environment has a huge impact on our productivity and effectiveness. Nobody understands that better than me, especially after two days sitting at a desk by myself! It's interesting at the moment to see how the rise of activity-based working is affecting workflow in organisations. If you're used to sitting with your team every day, a change to the office plan might make you feel more disconnected from them. On the other hand, if you're suddenly placed among a group of chatty people in an open-plan environment, you might find yourself struggling to concentrate. The environment we work in makes a big difference to how we feel about work.

Methodology

In a highly regulated environment such as finance, there are many established processes and procedures that must be followed. If you like following processes and don't feel the need to change them, that's great. You'll plough through the work in a really efficient and likely meticulous way. On the other hand, if you prefer to explore options and alternatives, then these processes will feel restrictive and you won't be able to operate at your best. Luckily, despite the regulatory environment we operate in, the world of finance is transforming significantly and opportunities often exist to change the way we approach and enforce organisational processes.

Depth preference

Your depth preference pattern, which falls on a scale from high in breadth to high in depth, relates to the level at which you prefer to think. If your breadth pattern is high, you prefer to look at the bigger picture and think strategically. Conversely, someone who is high in depth typically loves getting into the detail. Whilst we often need to go from the detailed transaction level to the market movement in a matter of minutes, we each have a preference.

Attitude toward change

This is simple: Do you like lots of change, change only for improvement's sake, or no change at all? As with all the preferences measured by iWAM, there is no wrong answer. It is all about assessing how your preference applies within your workplace, and whether it serves you or slows you down. If your department is transforming rapidly (and I don't know many areas of finance that aren't) and you don't like change, you will find it hard to give it your all. In contrast, if you love change and you're in charge of monthly financial reporting, well… you get my drift.

Point of reference

I find this set of patterns is particularly relevant for the women I work with. If you have a strong internal reference point, you generally know in your gut what's right or wrong. You are confident in your decisions and don't rely on feedback from others. Given that a lack of confidence is one of the three core reasons women in finance come to work with me, this measurement can be telling. On the other hand, external stakeholder engagement is a very beneficial leadership skill (and, as we discuss later in the book, a necessary part of your powerbase strategy), so a high external reference pattern can be very useful for women in finance.

It's important to understand that motivation and capability are not the same thing and don't always align. Motivators are about what revs you up, whereas capability is about what you are 'able' to do. We can easily see the difference in the context of the depth and breadth patterns. Among senior female finance leaders, we often see a much higher breadth pattern and a lower depth pattern. Often when I mention to someone that 'you don't like working with detail', they respond with something like, 'But I work with detail all the time – it's a massive part of my job.' That may be okay for now, and yes, these women are certainly *capable* of doing the detailed work – but it's not what they'd prefer to be doing. And while they might be able to bang out the detailed analysis meeting after meeting in the short term, ultimately they will start to feel so drained and demotivated by this 'grunt work' that their performance will start to slip. Why? Simple. Because their work is not in line with their subconscious motivators. In the long term, working against your motivators will harm your performance.

> A client of mine, Jennifer, came to me when she'd had enough of sitting in Stage 2A of the journey model. She had hit Point C, where she was clearly ready to take the steps she needed to thrive. Jennifer could feel her performance dropping as her motivation

continued to slip away and it needed to stop. Our sessions were transformational to her. When we ran the full iWAM profile on her, it was really clear that her current work activities were completely misaligned with her preferences. She loves change and innovation, yet in her current Financial Controller role she was responsible for the month-end process, which was far from exciting for her. She also works best in a group environment, however recent structural changes within the organisation meant that not only were there a reduced number of people in her team, she was left sitting on a floor away from the ones that did remain. We also identified that she loves big picture strategic thinking, and one of her key reflections was that she hadn't been using this talent lately. Learning this information (and much more!) was game changing. The friction and frustration she'd been feeling made sense. Very quickly, she identified changes that she could incorporate into her work: yes, she can't do much about the month-end process, but she could demonstrate her strategic thinking and previous experience in business partnering into her meetings, and be more proactive in sharing her strategic and innovative ideas. Within our first couple of sessions, and with this newfound knowledge of her motivators. she was able to make some substantive shifts in how she approached her work, which left her feeling far more fulfilled and effective.

The link between motivation and perception

It's important to note that our highest preferences represent not only the way *we* experience work, but also the way people experience *us* at work. Think on that for a minute. Each of us has a sense of who we are and how we want people to perceive us. We call this our identity. But more often than not, the way we perceive ourselves is not completely consistent with the way others perceive us. And when we're trying to make an impact at work, or influence others, or take the next step in our career, knowing how others perceive us (and how that differs from what we might have thought) is incredibly important.

Say you want to be perceived as a leader who empowers her team, thinks strategically, and communicates effectively. You use the iWAM tool, and learn that your highest patterns indicate that you have a tendency to micro-manage, are highly detail-oriented, and are quite blunt in your communication. Now that you know this, you can take action to bridge that perception gap. Far better to start to change how you are perceived now than after that attractive promotion has been given to someone else!

I'd love to give you an opportunity now to begin to motivate to accelerate. In a notepad, or on your laptop, draw the following table:

	GROUP	INDIVIDUAL	PROCEDURES	OPTIONS	BREADTH	DEPTH	DIFFERENCE	CONTINUOUS IMPROVEMENT	SAMENESS	INTERNAL	EXTERNAL
	Environment		Methodology		Depth preference		Attitude toward change			Point of reference	
Me											

If you prefer to print it off, you can also download this template from my website at: www.alenabennett.com.au

Now, ask yourself the following questions and place ticks in the appropriate spaces in the table.

- *Environment:* Do I prefer to work in a group (tick under 'Group'), or by myself (tick under 'Individual')?

- *Methodology:* Do I prefer to follow well-established procedures (tick under 'Procedures'), or do I prefer to brainstorm options and alternatives (tick under 'Options')?

- *Depth preference:* Do I prefer high-level, strategic thinking (tick under 'Breadth') or do I prefer working with details (tick under 'Depth')?

- *Attitude toward change:* Do I love change and thrive when I never know what the next day will hold (tick under 'Difference')? Do I like change but only when it's for improvement's sake (tick under 'Continuous improvement')? Or do I prefer to stick to the status quo – why change what's not broken (tick under 'Sameness')?

- *Point of reference:* Do I trust my gut (tick under 'Internal') or do I prefer to ask others to contribute (tick under 'External') before reaching a decision?

The key with answering these questions is to actually *decide* upon your preferred option – no fence sitters allowed! 'Every day is different, I like the variety' isn't helpful (except for the 'attitude toward change' question!). In order to get the most from this activity, you need to carefully consider what you'd prefer if you had the choice.

Once you have completed the table, use it to determine how your preferences align – or not – with your work on a day-to-day basis. Identify the areas of alignment and misalignment, and write them down. Now, for the misaligned areas, ask yourself:

❏ Do I like these areas of my work?

❏ What would it take to align these areas with my preferences?

❏ Whom do I need to talk to in order to reassign or align these areas of work?

Already you have some great actions to take towards making your work more efficient, more effective, and more fulfilling. Now for part two: Add some extra rows below 'Me': 'My team', followed by at least three critical team members.

Ask yourself the previous questions as it relates to each of these team members, based on your experience working with them. If you can't hazard a guess, simply put a question mark in the relevant column.

	GROUP	INDIVIDUAL	PROCEDURES	OPTIONS	BREADTH	DEPTH	DIFFERENCE	CONTINUOUS IMPROVEMENT	SAMENESS	INTERNAL	EXTERNAL
	Environment		Methodology		Depth preference		Attitude toward change			Point of reference	
Me											
My team											
1											
2											
3											

Once you have completed that activity for your team, ask yourself the following reflective questions:

❏ Were you able to make a reasonable attempt at guessing their preferences?

❏ Is the work they are responsible for in line with their preferences?

❏ How similar or different are their preferences to each other? To your preferences?

❏ How does the variation in preferences manifest itself in your team dynamics? How does that contribute (or not) to your team cohesion?

What does completion of this short activity tell you?

I expect you now have a list of actions that will not only contribute to your individual effectiveness, but also of that of your team members and your team as a whole! This is the power of knowing your motivators: you can take practical *and* tactical action that will accelerate performance.

> Doing this work at a team level produces some really interesting and productive conversations. Let me take you through the story of a finance leadership team I did this work with. One particular pattern was particularly insightful for the leader: Her 2IC's profile indicated that he held quite strong points of view when making decisions. Knowing enough about iWAM to know that she should be seeing this come through in his behaviour, she was really curious why that wasn't the case. In the team workshop we held after the individual profiles were done, she asked him exactly this. He said, "Well, I don't really think you want our opinions, and sometimes it's just easier to go with what you want." It doesn't take a rocket scientist to know that this feeling isn't ideal within a team! Ultimately, it provoked a really constructive discussion about how both the leader and her team should be communicating. They acknowledged and agreed that hearing differing points of view was critical if they were to be the 'proactive facilitators of high performance' that they strove for.

If you want to deliver results beyond the numbers immediately, figuring out what motivates you on a subconscious level should be your first step. By making the subconscious conscious, you can operate at a more tactical level. It's like having an additional set of levers in your leadership control tower that you can pull and push to make you and your team more effective at work. But beyond the work itself, beyond the allocation of tasks and resources, it's when a client says, 'Oh, now I understand why doing that part of my job drives me crazy!' or 'Yeah, I see that play out at work all the time. I would never have thought about it that way, but now I see why I'm getting these results' that I know things are falling into place for them. They now have a far deeper understanding of how they operate in their workplace, and with this knowledge comes power. I think for most of them there's a certain validation that comes with seeing the results come through in a highly validated statistical tool, especially in the language iWAM uses. There's a lightbulb moment where they realise, 'Now I get it, and it's okay. I'm okay.'

'I'm okay.' These two small words tell us so much about what is going on with many women in finance. Subconsciously, even the most confident, senior leaders are searching for validation – to fit in, to meet others' expectations. So when we discover all this information about ourselves, we feel a sense of peace, because we finally understand what's going on and why we feel as we do. And again, by taking the implicit and making it explicit, we can own it. We can actively make the changes necessary to increase our impact at work, whether that's about how we allocate tasks among the team, how we go about making decisions, or how we communicate with certain stakeholders.

Knowing what motivates you not only allows you to be more effective and fulfilled at work immediately, it also provides you with a huge amount of information that will enable you to start to identify your purpose. Purpose is a big concept and, to be honest, as long as you're juggling a demanding full-time job and responsibilities outside work, actively 'finding your purpose' is all but impossible. Instead, work on finding some strategies you can implement now to boost your motivation. When your work is aligned with your motivators, your sense of purpose will begin to emerge naturally.

2 REMOVE YOUR MASK

> "By trying to fit in, I was strengthening the culture that made me feel like I didn't fit in"
>
> *Melinda Gates*

How many times have you woken up in the morning and immediately dreaded the work day ahead? No sooner have you opened your eyes than you feel a pit in your stomach, like a tightly clenched fist. Or perhaps there've been times when you've woken up and had a delightful morning… until the moment you walk through the lobby doors. 'Oh, here I am again. Time to put on my mask.'

Wearing a 'game face' mask is an almost unavoidable part of being a woman in finance. More often than not, we assume this mask subconsciously. We might be the world's most outgoing, bubbly people person, who loves colour and smiling, who, God forbid, is actually quite feminine and 'soft' at heart… but when we walk through those doors, we become someone else. We assume a work persona that we have created because we believe it is the only way to fit in and succeed. Typically, this is a very masculine persona – one that does facts instead of feelings, and favours short, utilitarian conversations over shows of support… especially to other females in the workforce. My husband calls this my 'bulldog'! (Lovely, I know!)

Why do we do this? We do it because we're afraid of what being ourselves might mean. We do it to protect ourselves. Whether we're intimidated as the lone female in the group, worried that our natural style won't work, or concerned our feminine qualities will be perceived as weak, the mask provides a shield from judgment and potential exclusion.

When we have a greater level of awareness about what drives us at a subconscious level, when we step back and recognise how valuable our contribution is, we don't have to wear this mask anymore. We know that we are perfectly fine as we are, and we no longer need the armour we have inadvertently been wearing through all these years working in a sea of men in pale blue shirts. This doesn't mean we turn up to work wearing inappropriate clothes that will completely alienate our team and stakeholders – you can keep wearing the same clothes as before! But wouldn't it be great if we didn't have to live with a split personality? If we could find a synergy between our 'best selves' at home and at work?

When we go deep on our motivators, we can really lean into our true persona. We can spend less energy making sure our mask is on and more energy making a difference at work. It's a no-brainer that this will increase your impact and effectiveness.

You're not operating in a bubble

This all sounds easy enough, but there are many factors that may make you feel uncertain about taking your mask off. The reality is, you don't operate in a vacuum. Adopting new information and changing your own approach is one thing, but you're part of a broader context, and that context is constantly changing.

Think back to where accounting was when you (well, most of you!) commenced your studies. You started off studying Australian Accounting Standards, but then came the whole IFRS project. Now you needed to learn all the major differences between the new AIFRSs and the AASBs. You had to get your head around the Income Tax Assessment Act and then further around tax consolidation when that came into play. Not only did you need to learn them yourself and understand the differences, you also needed to be able to effectively communicate that to your stakeholders and clients, and help them adjust to the transition.

More recently at an industry level, think about the Royal Commission into Misconduct in the Banking, Superannuation and Financial Services Industry ('Royal Commission'). The effect of the events preceding the Royal Commission, the tone set, requests made, and questions asked by Commissioner Hayne throughout the hearings led to an uneasy time for the industry and all employees and leaders effected. Now that the findings have been released and an aggressive timeline of implementation has been shared (more than 20 recommendations by the end of this year, another 50 commitments by mid-2020, and the rest by the end of 2020), the industry can brace for continued change as regulatory requirements and legislation also change to reflect the intent of the findings. Speaking of regulatory change and compliance requirements, where is the world of audit going, where independence and quality are continually under the spotlight, particularly in the European Region? Global financial markets continue to be turbulent, as they react and respond to the many political, environmental and social stressors around the world. Cost pressures across the entire financial services industry have also been compounded by record low interest rates just as global growth shows signs of slowing. Uncertainty around the unwind of a decade of unprecedented central bank policy as well as divisive politics and a surge in protectionism further cloud what world we will leave the next generation of leaders. The macro world around us is constantly changing.

Let's now think more locally. What organisation isn't amid some sort of transformation at the moment? Whether it's a system implementation, an improvement program, or activity-based working, at a practical, day-to-day level we are constantly exposed to change. And we're expected to simply adapt to it, in addition to our business-as-usual (BAU) workload.

With all this change, it's easy to become stressed. And when we're stressed, it can feel more comfortable to leave our mask on. The stakes are higher during periods of intense change, and you don't want to stand out for the wrong reasons. So it's easier just to be a chameleon, especially among all the perceptions and unconscious biases around women in finance ("Are they about to take time off to have a baby? Are they going to be too emotional or soft?"). No wonder it sometimes feels easier just to keep that mask on.

Our brain is hardwired to flee from stress. When the metaphorical lion is glaring at us, we ready ourselves to run. It's easy to become overwhelmed by it all and say to yourself, 'I just need to wait this out and figure out what I want when it all settles down.' But you know what? That is a massive mistake, because it's never going to settle down.

Recently I was talking to a CFO about when we should start work together. He said, 'Maybe we should wait until the new year, so I can get this latest transaction complete.' And I said to him, 'Mike, with all honesty, there is no point waiting. Because we know that if we wait, something will always come up. Something always does.' And that's the truth. There is always something. Living in a world full of volatility, uncertainty, complexity and ambiguity (VUCA) is the new norm. Change is the constant. These catchphrases have become popular for a reason!

Unless we want to be bystanders to the change and watch the world move on without us, we need to accept that this is the new norm and lean into it. Embrace it. Excel in it. We need to know how to move from change cautious to change confident. Only then can we take that mask off permanently.

From change cautious to change confident

Let's now take a look at what characterises the change cautious and change confident approaches.

Change cautious

We become change cautious when the uncertainty and lack of clarity are so overwhelming that we go into a kind of threat state. We become very risk averse, avoiding action in favour of waiting to just 'see what happens'. When we are change cautious we are reactive – we fight fires, rather than preventing them. We don't plan ahead, and things spiral out of our control very quickly. How this manifests in our behaviour is that we (often unintentionally) demonstrate destructive behaviours. This may be as simple as asking questions that don't move a conversation forward, or being slow to turn tasks around simply because we're second-guessing ourselves. Change cautious is us wearing our masks, making sure we're presenting a safe (and guarded) face to the world.

Change confident

This is us at our best. When we're change confident, we participate in the change, wholeheartedly adopt the change, and quite often suggest further changes to make things even better! When we are change confident, we stand at the front lines and engage in constructive conversations around change. We challenge what we think we need to challenge, and we accept when the difficult decisions don't fall our way. We step up and take a proactive approach to the change, because we know that this is more likely to result in a positive outcome. No one likes having change 'done' to them, and the best way to avoid that is to be part of the doing.

Our behaviours are a direct result of what's going on in our heads. *Our mindset controls our behaviours.* So when we're change cautious, we react to uncertainty or change by asking, 'What does it mean for me?' We immediately think about the consequences, the challenges, the constraints. On the other hand, when we are change confident, our mind interprets change as an opportunity. Our behaviour is constructive – constantly asking, 'How do we make this change work for us?'

In her book, *Mindset*, Carol Dweck explores in depth the concepts of Growth vs Fixed mindsets. She explains that a fixed mindset is one that typically values accuracy and approval and that someone with a fixed mindset believes that when those are achieved, then you've succeeded. Conversely, someone with a fixed mindset also assumes that errors and disapproval are signs of failure. It's very black and white. When you think of how performance is measured at work, does that sound familiar to you? On the other hand, she explores the characteristics of someone with a Growth mindset. Someone with this mindset is focused on – yes, you've got it – growth and development. If you have a growth mindset, you think of possibilities and how to make the impossible possible (she cites Christopher Reeve as a classic example of this). People with growth mindsets want to find problems, because if you can find them, so arises the opportunity to solve them! Again, I think about how problem solving is such a key part of the job and so this theory has so much application for women in finance. If you can consciously adopt a growth mindset, then you have the foundations to operate above the line and be change confident.

Getting change confident

Using the definitions above, ask yourself:

What does change cautious look like to me?

In order to answer this question, I'd like for you to think about a time when you were going through a change that you <u>didn't like</u>, preferably in the context of your work. It can be as simple as moving from a private office to an open-plan working environment.

Now answer the following questions:

1. When I was going through this change, what was I thinking? What was going on in my head?

2. When I was going through this change, what did I notice about my behaviour?

This second question might be hard to answer at first. We're all adults, so I'm guessing you didn't walk around kicking and screaming. But you may have demonstrated some behaviours that are unlike you. Maybe you were impatient or snappy. Or perhaps you didn't participate in conversations as you usually would. Change-cautious behaviours often manifest as an absence of constructive behaviours, which can in itself be destructive and even toxic. So think deep on this, and be honest as you write down your answers.

Now ask yourself:

What does change confident look like to me?

In order to answer this question, think about a time when you were going through a change that you <u>did like</u>. This might be a change that you initiated or that you were active in steering – for example, improving a reporting process to provide greater insight to your stakeholders. Ask yourself the same questions as above:

1. When I was going through this change, what was I thinking? What was going on in my head?
2. When I was going through this change, what did I notice about my behaviour?

Get really specific about this second question, describing the images you see in your head in as much detail as you can. Are you standing? Are you smiling? How expressive are you? How are you interacting with your team, your boss, your family?

Now I'd like you to lean away from the page for a moment and review all the characteristics and attributes you've written down. Where do you think you stand right now? Many of you will likely admit that you are a bit change cautious, but hopefully you're ready to take steps to rip off the mask and be more change confident.

Now for the final part of this activity. Ask yourself:

In order to move from change cautious to change confident and keep that mask off, what do I need to do?

This is key. Because let's face it, we are all change cautious at times. The power of this activity lies in quickly identifying when we are being change cautious, and equally quickly transitioning to become more change confident. The challenge is that when we're stuck in change-cautious land, our judgment is generally not great and our thinking may be already clouded. We need a step-by-step guide to becoming change confident. That's what this part of the activity is about.

Ask yourself:

1. What are the thought processes or patterns that I need to step through in order to move my mindset from change cautious to change confident?

2. What are the things I need to do differently in order to change my behaviours from change cautious to change confident?

Now, you might find that it's hard to distinguish between mindset and behavioural changes here. And I get that – they are inextricably linked. But while behavioural change is hard (and sustained behavioural change is even harder), changing our mindset is hardest of all. It would be lovely to think that we could change our mind and simply let the behaviour follow, but it just doesn't work that way. We live in an action-oriented, results-focused world where it's what we do that counts. That's why I often encourage my clients to focus first on doing the behaviours, practising them, and allowing the results of those behaviours to reinforce their value and gradually change our mindset. We are what we repeatedly do.

After completing this activity, you should now have an image of yourself (represented in words) when you are change confident, and another of when you are change cautious – how you're thinking and what you're doing in each case. You can now use this awareness to identify when you are slipping below the line and away from your desired state. This in turn can give you the confidence to permanently remove that mask. Because when we're change confident, we don't need to fake it. We don't need to hide behind masculine traits. We can truly be in control of our own state and brand at work! Now that you understand this, you can take the action you need to move above the line and into a change-confident state.

> "Opening yourself up to growth makes you more yourself, not less"
>
> *Carol Dweck*

The key with this chapter is to recognise that context is king. We need to be aware of the context we are working in, and the impact that context can have on us. We live in a context of constant change, and we are going through that change with a population of people that are, for the most part, quite unlike us.

So let's get in front of it. Let's proactively adapt our mindset and behaviours to our context so that we can thrive as *us*, not a version of us behind a mask. Let's *participate* in creating a change that will help the women that come after us to ride the wave far more easily.

So we can remove our mask for good.

3 PLAN FOR PURPOSE

> "As a child, I never thought about what I wanted to be, but I thought a lot about what I wanted to do. As sappy as it sounds, I hoped to change the world."
>
> *Sheryl Sandberg*

At this point you might be thinking, 'Okay, great, I've got some great information about myself now. I know what gets me going, what revs me up.' Maybe you're realising, 'I know how to get myself out of that state of fear about the change going on around me. I don't need to let the busy-ness of business overwhelm me into a lesser version of myself.' You're probably feeling pretty damn good about yourself right now, and that's awesome. Go girl! That's exactly my intent. To make you strong.

At that same time, you're probably starting to wonder…

What now? Yes, incorporating some incremental changes into my working conditions might make it a bit less painful. But those changes won't be easy – I've worked here for a while now, and they know 'me'. How are they going to take it if I change? Work is hard enough right now. Maybe it's easier just to keep the status quo. I'm not sure the effort required to make these changes is worth it in the long run – I mean,

I don't even know how much longer I'll be here. I can't get past the feeling that I'm just not achieving anything. It's like there's something missing. It feels so meaningless going from meeting to meeting, feeling like all I do is talk with nothing meaningful to show for it. It's all a bit unfulfilling really.

Sound familiar? Maybe you also feel as if you're always trying to justify yourself and 'the numbers' to someone, whether it's your boss telling you that the numbers are wrong or a client who's furious about a new accounting or regulatory standard. It's all just a function of a bunch of assumptions on a spreadsheet, isn't it? What does it really all mean? Whose lives are you actually making better by doing what you're doing? What difference can one bean counter make, after all?

How can you get past this mindset? How can you use the data, attributes, and practical actions you've learned to transform the way you approach your work? As a woman in finance, operating in a male-dominated environment, how can you be a change maker for women in finance to come? How do you make your actions count?

We make actions count through purpose

Have you ever found yourself feeling awkward while talking about yourself during family functions, beers and barbies with friends, or when you pass someone on the street whom you haven't seen in a few years? Why is introducing yourself and talking about what you do so hard? You feel this way because over time, life has happened. You've celebrated achievements and setbacks, pleasure and pain, and your idea of what's important has gradually changed. You're starting to realise that you want to be more than just a 'finance person' – but you don't know how else to describe what you do.

You're probably familiar with Simon Sinek's book, *Start with Why*, or at least the TED talk of the same name. He famously says, 'People don't buy what you do, they buy *why* you do it[9].' He's talking about *purpose*. When we talk about making it all count through purpose, we're talking about asking and answering our own big *why*. That big, scary, overarching, meaning-of-life question. The one you may never have thought to ask yourself until now – or perhaps the one you've consciously avoided out of fear of the unknown.

Purpose is so important, because once you've discovered it, everything else falls into place. It forms the narrative behind everything you do – the *what* and the *how* in Sinek's famous 'Golden Circle' model. It creates those 'Oh, I get it' moments that immediately provide a sense of calm and control. Finding your purpose is the difference between moving without awareness or attention to operating with intention and reflection. It's a little like the difference between trying to get to the other end of a pool by floating lazily on your back versus doing freestyle straight down the pool.

Sinek explores that the 'why' comes from our *limbic* brain – one of the most ancient structures in the brain. This part of the brain is responsible for emotion, motivation, and fundamentally human behaviour. However, it has no capability for language. That's why matters of purpose or deep conviction can be so hard to justify or put into words – because they're driven by a part of your brain that doesn't do words! Language is the domain of our *neocortex*, a more highly evolved part of the brain that is also responsible for analytical reasoning and decision making. In finance, this part of the brain gets a serious workout! In finance – and most areas of life! – we must have words to support our decisions. It's no wonder we tend to focus more on our head and less on our heart (emotional brain).

In the next chapter, I'm going to take you through the process of identifying your purpose. It's not easy, it can be confronting, and it will get you thinking about your job in a way you never have before. But don't run away! This is where the magic happens. This is the moment you realise that meaning matters. This is the moment you realise your contribution to the world extends far beyond the numbers. This is the moment where it all makes sense.

So let's get started!

Most women in finance face many moments of 'exposure', and what I mean by that is moments where they can shine. When there's a specific milestone or deadline, it's easy to for them to identify their goal or aim. And when they achieve that goal, they're thrilled and energised. They finally feel a release of all the adrenaline that was pumping through their body as they worked through the project. Before my coaching sessions, to encourage reflection and aid preparation, I ask my clients six questions. The last question (or, rather, statement) is 'These are the three core needs I have for this coaching session.' Sometimes, this section comes back blank. And when it does, I know exactly what's going on.

When this section comes back blank, it means that my client doesn't know what they want. Think about that for a moment. How can you do a great job if you don't know what you want? Knowing what you want mobilises you into action and gives you a sense of direction, a destination to move towards. It enables progress. If you don't know what you want, you don't know where you're going. And that means you'll be stuck right where you are, spinning in circles. You will find yourself stagnating in stage 2A for a long time. Worse still, you will spend your time doing what others want, and how disempowering is that? It's like the saying goes: 'Build your own dreams, or someone else will hire you to build theirs.'

How can we end up working so hard every day… without a purpose? Usually it's for a combination of reasons. It may be that the release and relief we experience after achieving a milestone is so profound that we fall into a kind of lull. Our mind is clear for the first time in a long time, and we don't have the capacity to think about further growth. Downtime after deadlines is important, so this is okay for a while, but we can't let downtime turn into dead time. Alternatively, it may be that we feel so overwhelmed we can't see a way out.

But perhaps the biggest reason is the one that sits in between these extremes. When we immerse ourselves in our jobs, we get on the hamster wheel and do what we need to do to get through each day. When we are starting out, we do this because we need to prove ourselves. As time goes on, we continue to do it this way because we've created an expectation within ourselves – and others – that this is how we operate. So we just continue to do and do and do, never really lifting our head up to ask *why*. We get recognised, we get opportunities, and we make our way up the corporate ladder. And as the high-performing women in finance we are, we just keep on going.

Introducing Imposter Syndrome

But at some point we start to question how we got to where we are. And with that question inevitably comes self-doubt: *How did I end up here?* When there is no meaning behind our work – when we are operating without purpose – we fail to recall our achievements because we don't really see them as such. We don't recognise the brand we've created for ourselves at work, because we haven't created it purposefully. Before we know it, we're questioning whether we're even qualified to do this job! Other people's praise and positive perceptions only serve to increase the pressure to perform (while also fuelling the doubt that we can). This, my friends, is classic *imposter syndrome*. Imposter syndrome is the sense that you're faking it – that you're in a job you're not qualified for. When we feel fake, not only do we lose our confidence, we also feel shallow. This exacerbates our feelings of purposelessness… which then perpetuates our confidence issue. So begins a vicious cycle.

This is why purpose is so important. It sets our direction and fuels our momentum. It gives meaning to what we do and helps us persevere through the hard times. When we find our direction, we avoid allowing our performance or energy to plateau. We emerge fresh, with renewed energy and excitement. But finding purpose is like finding a needle in a haystack. It can seem easier to just walk away. But nothing good ever came easy. We need to acknowledge that our brain needs to go through some steps, some processes, to land on the purpose that is most meaningful to us.

> I'd like to share with you the story of one of my beautiful clients, Anneke. Her boss had asked her to work with me after she expressed concerns about feeling dissatisfied upon returning from maternity leave. She had decided to come back part-time and was struggling to reintegrate into the business, despite having been well established before taking time off. Her boss was understandably concerned about losing her, given that she was his 2IC.
>
> Anneke told me a bit about herself, both at work and at home. Eventually, she mentioned that she was thinking about changing her job title. When I asked her what it was currently, her hesitation was palpable. Finally she told me: 'Financial Controller.' She was desperately uncomfortable with the title, she said, because she felt she didn't live up to it: she felt like an imposter.
>
> Over the first couple of coaching sessions, we worked through her subconscious motivators and her purpose. Out of those sessions came insights more powerful than either Anneke or her boss could have foreseen. She realised that her purpose in life was to help women make better financial decisions, and that part of this was to assist in their financial literacy. When she said this, her face lit right up. As tears started to well up in her eyes, we knew we'd struck gold!
>
> Next we began to explore her current role in the context of her newly discovered purpose. As a financial controller responsible for a number of business units, her role was to help the business units make responsible financial decisions in order to achieve

their performance metrics. Boom! Link made between purpose and job. She was astonished at this finding! Immediately after our session, and over time, she found that her conviction in her job skyrocketed. She was turning things around more quickly, not hesitating in decisions, and engaging better with her team and stakeholders. Her performance indicators were amazing!

As for Anneke's boss, he was truly relieved to hear the insights she had gained and to see the conviction with which she now talked about her role. The clarity she had found around what she truly cared about in her work meant they could talk together about meaningful projects she could be assigned, safe in the knowledge that she wasn't going anywhere soon.

Doing this deep work to identify purpose is not about empowering women in finance to up and leave their jobs. In fact, it is completely the opposite. It is to empower women with the knowledge and understanding that their work matters, that they are making a contribution to the world through their current work, and that they are recognised and valued. It is to empower women with the capabilities to achieve their vision so that they have everything they need to be the change they want to create. Finally, it is to empower women with the confidence to know that they can achieve their dreams by building their own pathway there.

"Happiness is when what you think, what you say, and what you do are in harmony."

Mahatma Gandhi

3.1 META ACTIVITY 1: CONNECT TO YOUR PURPOSE

Up to this point we've looked at our motivation, our mindset, and why it's so critical we find our meaning. Often we get so caught up in the busyness of our day-to-day grind that we gradually lose our sense of self, until one day we wake up and wonder, 'Who am I?' Understanding what motivates us is key to improving our awareness of ourselves.

It's also useful to remember that our most powerful motivators happen at an intrinsic, not extrinsic, level – so rewards and carrots don't cut it in the long run. Focusing solely on getting to the next rung on the career ladder may work in the short term, but you risk feeling perpetually unfulfilled as you continually look for the next step, always wanting more. In the long run, the constant focus on climbing starts to feel monotonous, exhausting, and shallow. Not only that, but in today's world, where company hierarchies are flattening out and the number of 'rungs' is decreasing, if that's your only ambition then becoming stagnant is not a question of if, but when.

In fact, in the context of rapidly changing organisations, industries, and markets, it's never been more crucial to understand what mindset and behaviours we need to adopt in order to succeed. Having the awareness and flexibility to manage ourselves through this change means we can make sense of ourselves no matter what context we find ourselves in. It all starts with understanding the role of purpose.

It's time to do the deep work of building your connection to your purpose. You need to do this internal work before you can start pushing your impact out into the workplace and into the world. A common misconception about purpose is that once you know yours, you're set. There are hundreds of books, programs and experts on finding your purpose. We've all been given the sage advice, 'You just need to find your purpose.' But the thing is, just *finding* your purpose isn't enough.

Using your purpose

Purpose is something that needs to be followed and acted upon. It is not a destination in and of itself. Seeing it as such turns it into a kind of nirvana, something you can never actually achieve or make any progress towards – which is even more frustrating than not having a purpose at all! It's like being given a taste of something divine (truffles, anyone?), then having it snatched away from you. As the cravings intensify, you start to wish you'd never tasted it to start with! You also risk meeting the shadow of purpose: procrastination. This is where you ask "why" to everything with such frequency that you get stuck into paralysis by analysis and can't move forward. Have you ever spent an hour with a 5 year old? Why? Why? Why? It's exhausting!

When you find your purpose, you need to work out how it does or doesn't align with your activities at work. But you need to be very careful about how you do this. If you make a snap judgment that your purpose doesn't align with your job (which is easy to do because, let's face it, whose purpose involves spreadsheets and financial reports?), your brain will immediately begin seeking evidence to support this conclusion. It will consistently and continually send you further messages that the work you're doing is out of line with your purpose until you end up feeling that your work is useless and your life has no meaning. So how can you stop this from happening? You need to know how to *use* your purpose once you've found it. That's what this first meta activity is all about – bringing together the different levels of your purpose to make a real impact.

The three layers of purpose

A common challenge women in finance face around purpose is that they don't know what to do with it. It sits 'out there', an intangible nirvana with no place in the very rational world we operate in. To work out how we can actually *use* our purpose, we must always address three layers:

- *Strategic* layer: This is the big-picture stuff – the long-term view of what we're doing and why.

- *Tactical* layer: This is where we dig into *how* we're going to achieve the goals we identified in the strategic layer – what tactics we're going to deploy.

- *Practical* layer: This is what we're going to do now!

Purpose: The strategic layer

Vision

The first thing we need identify is our vision.

What do you want your career to look like over the next 3–5 years?

As you're asking yourself this question, check off the following more detailed questions:

- ❏ What problems do I want to be solving?
- ❏ Do I want to be leading people?
- ❏ How big an organisation do I want to be working in?
- ❏ Where do I want my job to be located (geographically)?
- ❏ What level do I want to be at? What role to do I want to have (if known)?
- ❏ How much money do I want to be making?

Answer these questions objectively and without presumption, expectation, or bias. Forget about how you are going to get there! Or, if it helps, work on the basis that you definitely will.

This is not about identifying whether or not you want to stay in your current job. The last thing I want is for you to make a hasty decision that you may regret. I do not want a mass exodus from organisations because of these activities! This is about objectively identifying the characteristics of your career – at some point in the future – to serve as somewhat of a compass. I've chosen 3–5 years as the timeframe because I often find that beyond that point people struggle to make it feel 'real'.

Values

What are the top three to five values that are non-negotiable for you in your career?

Think about where you work, the people you work with, and the characteristics of the role. Common values I see with women in finance are integrity, accountability, humility, teamwork and growth, but there are any number of others that may be most relevant for you. At this stage of your career, you probably have a reasonable sense of your non-negotiable values, but I find it is always useful to check in with yourself and just confirm that this really is what you value in this moment. To sense-check whether they are the 'right' ones, think about how you live those values, or how you would like to live those values.

Are you a bit warmed up to this now? Because this is where it starts to get interesting!

Your edge

Ask yourself:

What are the unique talents and capabilities that set you apart from others in your area of expertise?

The challenge with this question is pinpoint what you do differently to anyone else you know. This question can be so powerful in and of itself.

> When I worked through the strategic layer exercise with Nat, a gorgeous financial controller, we spent probably 30 minutes just digging deep into this question. I asked her to identify three unique talents and capabilities that set her apart from others. And, like most people, she came up with three that were great, but not unique. In fact, I think her initial three were so full of business jargon that I couldn't even work out what she was trying to tell me! So we drilled down into what she meant: How are you doing this *differently*? Why do you think you get *better* results than others? Finally, it landed. Boom! Her edge was that she could think more strategically and initiate more effective outcomes for her organisation because she could incorporate both the financial control aspects of her current job (i.e. accounting standards and financial reporting) and her previous experience in the same organisation as a finance business partner (i.e. from a commercial perspective). Nat also had the communication agility that came with that experience, which meant she could be more intentional and impactful in her communication. The impact was profound. She had uncovered superpowers she hadn't even realised were in her toolkit and in doing so could bring finance to life! All that was left was to go back to work and let these flourish.

So use this question well. It's so very impactful.

Your eulogy

Now, before we get into this, I want to be clear: this exercise is *intended* to trigger emotion. And not because I'm a sadist! It's to help you connect your rational left brain to your emotional right brain, because this is the most reliable way to commit to long-term behaviour change. That's because it engages and connects the parts of our brain that are responsible for long-term memory and recall. When we find our purpose while triggering these parts of our brain, it is captured in our memory forever. That's why people say that when you find your purpose, things become easy – because you don't forget your purpose easily. It's always there. You don't need to 'try' to remember it. Give yourself the space and time to really lean into this part of the activity, and you will reap its full benefit.

Until now, we have focused on a period of 3–5 years from now. Now we are projecting all the way forward to after you have passed away. Your task is to write your eulogy – a tribute to your life in a few paragraphs. Write what you would *like* to be said about you, regardless of whether or not you're on track for that. The key to this exercise is to write using the 'stream of consciousness' method – write whatever you're thinking, and don't stop! Try to keep your pen to paper and not overthink it. (Just like when I wrote the draft manuscript for this book! My editor told me, 'Just keep writing, and I'll do the editing!')

Expect to start at a pretty simple place: 'Alena was a loving wife and mother of two gorgeous girls, Leilani and Mila…' And just let it flow from there. Let it go wherever you'd like it to go. I've had clients whose eulogies have included how they dressed and what lipstick they wore! So really, let it go wherever. Give yourself enough time to start to feel uncomfortable. And when you think you're done… give yourself a few more minutes. You've got this! When the tears start to drop onto the page, you know you're getting there.

Now you're ready to write your mission.

Mission

Describe your *why*. What difference or contribution do you want to make to the world through your career? This question floors many of the women I work with. They look at me in wonder, as if they've genuinely never thought about how a career in finance could contribute to the world. But – and this is why the order of activities in this layer is so important – after the initial shock, they realise that, actually, they *are* in the right headspace to consider a response.

Now ask yourself: What gets you excited about the impact you can have through your career? You should be starting to experience some feelings deep in your core. They've moved from your heart (in the previous activity) down to your stomach, and this is how you know that what you're identifying is real. It's deep. It's more than powerful, it's purposeful.

Purpose: The tactical layer

Metrics

Now that we have identified our mission, we need to get into the detail. We need to identify how we will know when we have achieved our mission – the metrics that we can measure and report on to tell us how we're going

The first step is to define your success. Ask yourself, 'What does success look like to me?'

The second step is to identify the metrics that will measure that success. These may be defined by time, performance, or any other metric that is meaningful to you.

The big question here is, 'How will I know I have achieved my mission?'

Your leadership style

In order to achieve success, whatever that means to you, I expect you'll need to 'level up' your leadership style. As Marshall Goldsmith says in his book of the same name, 'What got you here won't get you there[10].' To help us identify what your new leadership style looks like, we need to identify what you'd like your stakeholders to be saying about you. And we need to do this for all your key stakeholder groups.

1. Your boss: When you are in this future state, achieving your mission, how would your boss describe your leadership style?
2. Your team: When you are in this future state, achieving your mission, what would your team say they love about working in your team?
3. Your stakeholders: When you are in this future state, achieving your mission, why do your stakeholders value your contribution to their world?
4. Your peers: When you are in this future state, achieving your mission, how would your peers describe your contribution to the team?

How you capture your responses is up to you. You may like to simply list your responses under four separate headings, or you may prefer to draw up a quadrant graph (a big cross) and put a stakeholder group in each quadrant. Whatever works for you!

You should now be able to identify the common themes, overarching attributes, capabilities, and qualities that will form the basis of your ideal leadership identity.

This is the person you need to become in order to achieve your mission.

Your plan

We now have our purpose, our vision, and our strategy.

We also have a good sense of what success looks like, and what our leadership style needs to be in order to achieve it.

Now we need to get even more tactical and identify exactly *how* we are going to achieve it. I think this comes down to three key areas: capabilities/skills, relationships, and ways of working.

Now, because I am someone who loves to deliver results through people, I always start with relationships.

Relationships

What relationships do you need to have in place in order to achieve your vision? Imagine yourself at the peak of your career, as you are achieving your vision. Who are your key relationships with? Whom do you hang out with at work? Whom do you call when you need help?

My guess here is that you won't know the names of the people that you need to know. But you may know that you will need a network full of C-suites, from CEO to COO and everyone in between. You may know that you will need good relationships with the key market players and industry bodies, and the key public figures in those areas.

If you know their names, great! If not, just describe the roles as specifically as you can. So if you think you'll need to know around five CEOs, write that down: '5 CEOs from X industry.'

Skills and capabilities

When you are performing at your peak, you will be accessing a variety of skills and capabilities, both technical and non-technical. In finance, the technical aspect is critical, and proven success in this area is of fundamental importance as we get into those senior leadership roles. But I want to be clear here – it's the non-technical skills that set you apart. Anyone can learn technical, and everyone is expected to know technical. But you've already conquered technical. It's time to lift yourself out of the detail and move into tactical, non-technical skills.

So when you are identifying the skills and capabilities you'll be leveraging in your dream job, list all the technical and non-technical capabilities you think you'll be using the most. Don't include the technical capabilities of the team that will be 'doing the doing'. Focus on the ones that you will be using as the leader you described in "*Your leadership style*".

Ways of working

When I talk about ways of working, I don't just mean the everyday ways of working with your people and stakeholders. I'm also talking about the habits you've established for yourself.

Picture yourself in your dream job. Now tick of these questions as you ask yourself:

- ❏ How are my days structured?
- ❏ How do I work with my team?
- ❏ How often do I communicate with my team?
- ❏ What specific ways of working do I adhere to in order to perform at my best?
- ❏ Do I top and tail my days with 'meetings with myself' to plan and reflect? Or do I have sessions at the beginning and end of the week for that?
- ❏ How do I manage my other responsibilities? Do I work from home one day a week? Or do I start early or finish late on certain days so I can pick up and drop off the kids?
- ❏ What processes, systems and structures do I have set up across my week, and in every day, that makes me successful?

Making sense of your plan

You now have a strong idea all the important relationships, skills, and ways of working that you'll need when you're at your peak. Let's now bring those together in a simple table:

Nailing it	Have it, but could improve	Don't have it

Think about all the relationships, skills, and ways of working that you're already doing at the high level you would require in your peak state. Stick these in the 'Nailing it' column. Now consider which ones you have or are already doing, but that you know you need to 'lift' or improve. Stick these in the 'Have it, but could improve' column. Be honest about which ones you don't have, aren't doing at all, or don't even know where to start! Stick these in the 'Don't have it' column.

This is the transitional step, the moment where you begin to move from 'tactical' to 'practical'.

Purpose: Let's get practical!

Now that we've done all this great work to identify what we want long-term and how we can go about getting there, we need to bring it to life – *today*. In this way, we not only set ourselves up for success in the future, we also amplify our impact and improve our performance today, because we now know what revs us up and makes us most productive at work. We know the mindset and behaviours we need in this constantly changing context.

Reflecting on the work you have done so far, answer the following questions:

- ❏ What is the most important thing that will help you achieve your vision?
- ❏ How is the current context impacting that?
- ❏ What do you need?

- ❏ What is your key concern?
- ❏ What support do you need from your leaders?
- ❏ What support do you need from your peers?
- ❏ What support do you need from your team?
- ❏ What support do you need from anyone else?

Finally, to close off our work on connecting to your purpose:

What are the three actions you can take this week that will have the biggest impact on either (a) getting you to your desired peak state or (b) optimising your current work?

Congratulations!

You have discovered your purpose and made it practical! You should now be deeply connected to your purpose and have a clear understanding of how your current work contributes to your future vision and mission.

PART 2: ATTRIBUTES

4 OWN YOUR IMPACT

> "I now understand that life is a sequence of experiences and events that we create for ourselves in order to learn something from them."
>
> *Linda Buchan*

How many times have you read a book, listened to a podcast, or been in a training room and gotten really excited about the possibilities ahead, only to then walk into your office and think, 'Oh… back to reality. There's no room for that here'?

I've had a number of conversations recently with people in the finance industry who've done a coaching course and absolutely loved it. They've learned the powerful impact of coaching, and are energised to share their learning. Many of my clients have come out of multi-day training courses on really useful, practical skills feeling excited and motivated. But inevitably, they end up telling me, 'I just haven't been able to apply it properly in my current job.'

So often we fail to make the impact that we want. Why? Where does all this enthusiasm for new skills go? What happens to all our great intentions about the new program we're going to follow? Why do we fail to implement our great ideas?

I imagine that after reading through the first four chapters and completing the meta exercise at the end, you have all sorts of grand plans for how you are going to get to where you want to be. Having articulated your purpose and identified its key components and dependencies, I imagine you're pretty blown away by the opportunities you've now opened for yourself. But as you know, the number-one factor in the success of a new skill is whether you start applying it straight away. And that's great, because it reflects the fundamental premise of this chapter.

We must take 100% responsibility for our impact

Taking 100% responsibility includes our mindset, decisions, actions, and perceptions. We must own the work we choose to do today, the work we have chosen to do in the past, and the work we choose to do tomorrow. Because no one else can, and no one else will. It's on us. So when you do something – whether that's enrolling in training, or engaging a coach, or starting to attend networking events – you need to do it in a way that will benefit you *now*.

When you're surrounded by people that give you all sorts of inspiration, knowledge, and ideas about how you can achieve your purpose, your brain gets flooded with dopamine, which gives you a rush of pleasure and gets you motivated and energized. But then you walk out of that training room and into your office. Now the dopamine is replaced with cortisol – the stress hormone responsible for that tense knot in your stomach.

Your cortisol-flooded body must now try to navigate the question of how to maintain that inspiration and motivation, how to continue to take steps toward your purpose, in the context of an uninspiring day job that makes you feel disempowered. You want to take action, but all you can think is 'this is out of my control, and I can't make it better'. Suddenly it doesn't seem worth it anymore. And all your great learning, intentions, and actions get filed away in the bottom drawer while you focus on just getting through the imminent stress and deadlines at work.

The service myth

Finance is a services industry, a services function. And I think we have been sold a myth about service. We have been brought up to believe that being in service is about relinquishing control and letting someone else call the shots. This is a pretty easy assumption to make in finance, because numbers are, in and of themselves, a function of performance – performance that is usually driven by someone else. Even in a forecasting and budgeting scenario, it is usually not the finance person's job to make the performance happen. That's why finance is often perceived as back office, and why strategic business partnering can be so hard for some finance functions. But we need to bust this myth. We need to get ahead of the game.

Being in service does not mean being a servant. Women in finance are highly skilled professionals and have lots to offer. That's why we need to focus our attention and energy on being proactive, not reactive. This is how we take 100% responsibility for our impact. We become proactive. We become creators.

If we are proactive in our approach to everything we do, we will create the conditions we need to succeed, now <u>and</u> into the future. This is the foundation of Dr Stephen Covey's work, *The 7 Habits of Highly Effective People*[11]. In fact, it's habit number 1. He believes that 'our responsibility is our ability to respond' and states that, 'The proactive approach to a mistake is to acknowledge it instantly, correct and learn from it.' Actually, I'd take this quote one step further and say that the proactive approach to *anything* is to acknowledge it instantly, correct and learn from it. You don't need to make a mistake in order to be proactive. You can be proactive in so many aspects of your life.

You can be proactive about:

- A thought that isn't serving you
- An action that didn't yield the right outcome

- A behaviour that didn't receive the right response
- A response that you didn't like
- A relationship that isn't working

You need to own what is happening to you and around you.

I'd like to apply this concept in two areas that I think will be useful to you. Firstly, let's consider the timeless complaint that 'I don't have enough time!' This is the most common complaint I hear. It is also one of the biggest excuses people use to explain why they haven't achieved something (even when they don't need to make excuses!). You're probably expecting me to say, 'You actually have plenty of time. You're just not using it well. Become more productive!' Sorry to disappoint! I actually reckon this is a valid challenge for women in finance. Time is a finite resource; it is not renewable and, until time travel becomes possible, we cannot get it back.

Women in finance have a lot going on: they have their work, and they have their life. If they are mothers, they have the additional load that comes along with that – the logistics, the planning, the stress. Think about a moment when you were sitting around the meeting-room table brainstorming an issue and realised you and the team were in for a late night. If you have kids, chances are your next thought was 'Who's going to pick up the kids from daycare? What are they going to eat for dinner?' I know it's a complete stereotype, but in my experience, women are the only ones thinking like this. The reality is that for the most part, that mental load[12] rests with the woman. So as you sit around the table in full troubleshooting mode, you, as the only woman, are the only one simultaneously having to troubleshoot how to make this work for your family.

This pressure isn't exclusive to women with children. In fact, women without children have just as little time, their commitments simply look different. Women in finance tend to have numerous and diverse interests outside of work and, like all high performers, they are deeply committed to them. Whether it be running or crossfit, F45 or yoga, family or friends, a partner or the search for a partner, women in finance have full and complex lives. We simply cannot ignore the challenge of time. And that's why I'd like to explain how to apply the concept of proactivity to time, deadlines, and dates.

Imagine you've just been handed a tight deadline.

Your natural reaction is probably to go straight into reactive mode and adopt a 'scarcity mindset'. 'Oh my gosh,' you think to yourself, 'how on earth am I going to get it all done by then?' You look at your extended to-do list, which never seems to get any shorter; your calendar, which is already full for the next 2 weeks; and your understaffed team, who are already working long hours, and you think, 'I guess I'll just have to suck it up and make it happen.' When you start with this mindset, you're likely to approach the task with less energy and less motivation. You will probably do the bare minimum in the time you've got. Now, in certain situations, this can be a great tactic: the Minimum Viable Product concept involves doing the bare minimum in order to test a hypothesis. But in this case, it is not a tactic. It is a default behaviour, reflecting the 'reactive mode' you've slipped into.

Now imagine being given a deadline and being proactive about it. The context is the same – too much work, not enough time – but you get ahead of it by understanding more about the deadline and the deliverable. What is driving the timing? What is the purpose of the deliverable? You get the 'real story', and influence the timing and the work from there. The intent and focus of your line of inquiry is simple: you are being value driven about your work. You are focused on understanding the value of the work you've been asked to do, so that you can make better decisions about the way you spend your time. If you take this approach in all your work, you'll be doing the same or less work, but delivering more *value* (doing more targeted work).

Think about the impact this approach would have on your mindset. On how much control you feel over your work and your career. And, as a result, on your ability to effectively plan your time and invest your energy into bringing your vision to life through your work. *What impact would it have on your confidence levels?*

At this stage you might be thinking, 'I can't challenge deadlines! I can't ask those questions!' And I counter that with, why not? All you need to do is put the relationships in place to do so.

> When I moved to San Francisco and worked in the KPMG audit practice, I was really lucky with the first engagement I was put on. It was an SEC-listed company, so it certainly stretched me from a technical perspective. Not only did I have to contend with the US GAAP, I also had to quickly learn the practical application of the Sarbanes–Oxley Act (SOX). As if that wasn't enough, my manager was more than a little cynical about how good I'd be (she later told me she expected the worst, thinking that I was from a small island and likely had kangaroos as pets!). Fortunately, she gave me the benefit of the doubt. Both she and our engagement partner were really good about giving me great career opportunities. So I quickly found myself presenting to audit committees.
>
> There's one particular audit committee meeting I'll never forget! I was sitting in this meeting, and the CFO had just told us the date of the next meeting. Now, in case you've never been involved in such committees, you should know that the logistics of setting meeting dates are painfully complex, so much so that they are usually locked in about 12 months in advance. At this point, the partner said, 'I can't come to the next one; it's a Jewish holiday and I'll be taking my son to temple.' I was amazed and inspired at the same time, to think that he'd put a personal commitment in front of work so publicly and transparently. But I was also wondering how the CFO would react, as he was known to have a short fuse at times. 'Okay then, we'll change it,' the CFO responded.

From that day forward, I knew that 'if you don't ask, you don't get.' More to the point, if you do ask, you do get! And this applied even in the work context. I also know, after so many experiences before and after that one, that dates can almost always move. Even with the scary regulators! Just because someone says they 'are bound by regulatory deadlines' doesn't mean that deadline isn't moveable.

Ask. Speak up for yourself.

The second area I'd like to apply this concept is around relationships. Our ability to be confident in being proactive about timing depends upon the quality of the relationships we have.

Now, we all know that engagement with others is critical in our work. We can't do everything ourselves – we rely on other people to provide inputs, and we deliver the outputs to others for review, approval, and presentation. So we engage with people when we need something. But if that's the *only* time we engage with them, our relationships are limited to being purely *transactional*. (For those of you that work in the month-end or year-end financial reporting processes, can you think of people you converse with only at those times?) When I need you or you need me, we talk – but otherwise, no dice. There's no depth in these relationships, which means there's no room to leverage and influence for better outcomes.

When we are proactive in our relationships at work, we can leverage them. We can have influence and impact. When we are asked to do something we believe is wrong, unreasonable, or not valuable, we can have a conversation to determine what actually needs to happen in order to achieve an outcome that satisfies both parties. This is how you achieve a win/win – but in order to get there, you need to have the relationship in place first.

Opposite is a snapshot of the framework I have described above. You can see that we can describe the relationships we approach proactively as impactful, and those we approach reactively as transactional. On my website, you'll find a handy resource to help you identify which of your relationships are transactional and which are impactful.

You can access and download this resource at www.alenabennett.com.au

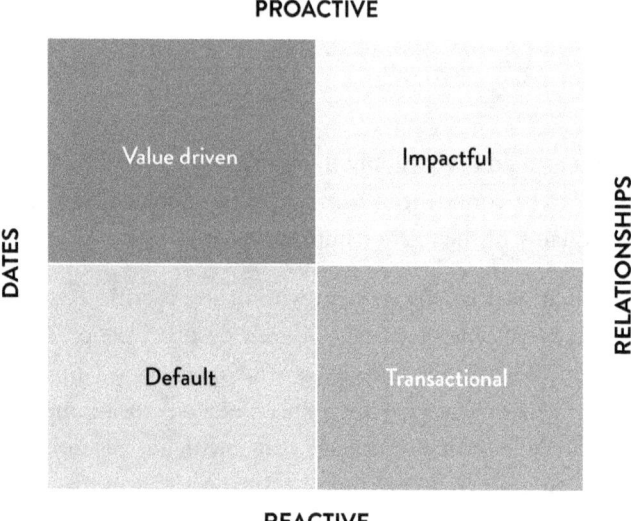

Now hold a mirror to yourself. Where do you need to take responsibility for your impact, and shift from being reactive to being proactive? Where are you not getting the results you want?

Use the following table to help you articulate this.

Desired results	Current results (undesired)	What is my current mindset, action, and behaviour around it?	What proactive action can I take to get the desired result?

I take a very proactive approach in the work I do with my clients. I think this is a key part of thinking strategically and achieving your goals. I believe that everything is possible, and nothing is really out of reach – you just need to be proactive about it.

I'm reminded of the time I influenced the date and time of my eldest niece's birthday party. I was looking the calendar, and noticed I had a few other commitments I wanted to keep around her birthday. So I said to my brother, 'When are you having Amira's party? What if we do it on this date, around this time?' It sounds cheeky, but I was actually doing him a favour. I'd done the thinking for him, when he hadn't thought about the party at all. And so he was able to simply answer, 'Yeah, sweet!'

Do the work. Be proactive. Get the results you want.

5 ESTABLISH YOUR POWERBASE

"You can do what I cannot do. I can do what you cannot do. Together we can do great things"

Mother Teresa

In the last chapter we looked at taking responsibility for our impact. We established that quality relationships empower us and increase our effectiveness and fulfilment at work. I mentioned earlier that the most common complaint I hear is about a lack of time. But most people find that when they work through the challenge using the model in the previous chapter, they realise that time isn't the problem – it's people. But the great thing is, while people are the problem, they are the solution, too. Relationships are one of the most important currencies for leaders today. But relationships are about more than just getting an extended deadline or time off work. Here, we're going to go much deeper into why we can't do it all alone.

This is what working alone looks like for a woman in finance. Check all the ones you recognise in your work:

❏ When you get a great opportunity, like being on the steering committee for a high-profile project, you don't have anyone to delegate your work to. Your to-do list just piles up, and you can't properly take advantage of the opportunity.

- ❏ When you're trying to build a strategy to hit a certain number within a specific timeframe, you don't have anyone to brainstorm and build ideas with.

- ❏ When you feel uncertain about your career or your future within your organisation, you have no female mentors to ask about their journey and any potential opportunities.

- ❏ When you need the skills or expertise of someone more senior in a different part of the organisation, or even if you simply need to ask them a question, you don't have anyone to help open that door for you.

- ❏ When you have to meet with someone senior for the first time, there's nobody you can ask to get the intel to set up your meeting for success.

In fact, the feeling of isolation that you get when you're working alone was summed up recently by a message I received from a senior female finance leader who said, 'It's been lonely operating like this for many years in Finance teams.'

And that's just the beginning. But the important thing to note is that women may choose to work alone for many reasons. It may be that:

- ❏ We feel that we don't need others' help.

- ❏ Delegation isn't our strong suit.

- ❏ Our colleagues treat us unfairly or make us feel uncomfortable.

- ❏ It seems easier to just get it done than to teach someone else to do it.

- ❏ We feel we've never been good at meeting new people.

- ❏ We feel that the people around us aren't able to give us the help we need.

- ❏ We're worried we will appear 'weak' if we ask for help.

Or it may simply be a matter of not knowing what to do and where to start.

People have an important place in helping us achieve our vision, and not just for their technical, 'how-to' skills. We will refer to the people that you rely on at work as your 'powerbase'. I prefer this term to 'network', as *powerbase* more explicitly indicates that the group of people that you have relationships with will strengthen your ability to achieve your vision.

We need people around us. Think about the story of Moana and all the people who helped her restore the heart of Tefiti. She was surrounded by so many important characters, who made up a pretty inspiring powerbase! She had Maui, of course: he knew where the heart was, and she needed him to teach her the skill of wayfinding. But she also had her late Gramma Tala, who shared with Moana her family history and the internal scars her dad was carrying, and gave her the courage to follow her mission. She had her mother, who helped her father through his fear of what might befall Moana out at sea. And – bless! – she had that crazy chicken Hei Hei to lighten things up on their journey!

We don't just need people around us – we need them to actually help us! A client of mine, Sarah, was sharing with me some of the challenges she'd been facing around getting in front of the right people to move her work forward. She gave me the lay of the land in terms of her relationships with people at work, including those stakeholders she wanted more time with. Even though I hadn't known Sarah long, I got the sense that she was someone people would enjoy talking with. I was struggling to see where her roadblock was, and I told her so. I asked, 'Would your boss take you along to a meeting or two to help you open up the doors?' The answer was a simple no. So there we had it. The person that knew her performance the best, who could be her biggest advocate, champion, and supporter, was instead doing quite the opposite.

We need a powerbase, and we need it to support us

Your powerbase allows you to make things happen. They are the ones that make the decisions, have access to additional or different resources and information, and can help you turn projects around more quickly. They are your activators. They activate ideas, people and most importantly activate you to do the things that make you your best. Many of us have built up our powerbase intuitively without even thinking about it, by simply establishing strong relationships with the people we interact with at work. Some of us even have a blind spot when it comes to building and nurturing professional relationships and so don't even know how important they are and the value they can provide. What I want to do in this chapter is show you how to be strategic and tactical in building your powerbase.

Having identified your purpose, you're now on a trajectory that you can't ignore. Because when you find your purpose, it tugs at you all the time. But if your purpose is big, bold and possibly a little scary – and I reckon it probably is – you might be thinking, 'How on earth am I going to achieve this?' This is where your powerbase comes in. Your powerbase is the group of people that will, step by step, person by person, open up the opportunities that will help you move closer to your vision. These are opportunities that don't even exist today. Your powerbase will *create* opportunities for you, because they want to see you succeed.

Your powerbase is critical to your career growth, because these are the people who will roll up their sleeves and pitch in to help you deliver to that crazy deadline. These are the people who will listen when you need to vent about something you've stuffed up at work. And these are the people who will give you the feedback and new ideas you need to hear in order to 'level up' and take the next step at work.

To build a powerbase that can support you in this way, you must take a proactive approach to your professional relationships. If you have completed the meta activity already, you will have identified some of the people you need to get to know in order to achieve your vision. But, unless you're into cold calling – and I've not yet met a woman in finance who is! – you will need your powerbase to help you with those introductions.

But first I want to dig a little deeper into why it's so important for *women* in finance to have a strong powerbase. I believe everyone needs a strong powerbase, but the context in which women operate means they often need more help to thrive. Finance is an ecosystem dominated by men and the resultant masculine legacy culture. It's not that men are resistant to helping women per se, but more that people naturally find it easier to help people who are more like themselves. This is called 'Sameness' bias[13]. It makes sense, then, that the fewer women there are in finance, the fewer people will feel naturally drawn to help women. This applies regardless of the type of help we're talking about – whether that's helping women get more opportunities, helping to shift perceptions around women in finance, or simply being an advocate for women in the workplace.

In his book, *Why Do So Many Incompetent Men Become Leaders?: (And How To Fix It)*[14], psychologist Tomas Chamorro-Premuzic pulls together the macro level statistics and draws provocative (but logical) conclusions from them. Such as, if we know that men outweigh women in senior leadership positions, and we know that most employees are disengaged at work, then we can draw the conclusion that male leadership is ineffective in many areas. He distinguishes between leadership qualities as "criteria that will predict actual performance rather than individual career success." We assume that the two are the same, but one is focussed on organisational performance and one is focused on the individual leader. The important point that I want to draw out from his work is that even though men are typically more confident, feminine leadership competencies like humility and emotional intelligence actually deliver better business results. Contrasting that with competencies like confidence, he admits "that we want them, but we don't necessarily need them."

More recently, the emergence of the #MeToo movement may have inadvertently given rise to additional complexities layered on this already challenging issue for women in finance. Investment Banker and international bestselling author, Katherine Tarbox, shared her insights in a 2018 article in the Harvard Business Review[15]. The premise behind her article was that despite the intent of the #MeToo movement being about the important diversity conversations (and resulting actions) that need to be taking place, what she was experiencing was quite the opposite. In fact, the overt and general nature in which sexual harassment was being discussed simply injected fear into the already unconsciously biased minds of men. This subsequently led to these men feeling that withdrawing from socialising with and hiring women in the work place would be the easier and safer course of action. Given that both actions serve to pull genders apart, and are based on incorrect and unvalidated assumptions around respect and trust, this does nothing to improve diversity and inclusion. If this is a new complexity that women in finance now need to deal with, then getting our powerbase in place is more important than ever.

A further interesting observation about women in finance is that sometimes they don't have each other's backs. This may or may not be intentional. I have seen and heard numerous examples of women in finance actively thwarting each other at work, whether that be by talking down about them, denying them opportunities even when they are due, denigrating them for making time for family commitments, or criticising her clothes. As if it wasn't hard enough already as a woman in finance to find role models in the organisation, some women actually find that the senior women in their organisations are the last people they'd turn to for help.

Wouldn't it be great to see the senior women in finance support and strengthen the other female trailblazers in the organisation? Don't senior women in finance have a responsibility to help emerging female leaders to flourish? Don't you think the lack of support among women in finance is part of the reason why female application rates into the finance world are so low? Do you see why we need to have a strong powerbase?

Whether you contribute to that behaviour or not (and, since you're reading, I hope you're not), I'm sure you'll agree that women are a tough crowd and often our harshest critics. Not that this is always intentional. We're a product of the system we're brought up in. If that system doesn't value women, we are less likely to value women, even if we are one! It's not just men who develop unconscious biases about how things are done. And in a male-dominated world, it's easy to forget about our very important role in actively promoting women in finance. Unless we're careful, we may inadvertently contribute to the ongoing lack of female representation in finance leadership roles by not being strategic and proactive about identifying and providing opportunities for women in finance.

Deciding what our powerbase should look like

One of the common mistakes women in finance make is to invest ourselves almost exclusively in our current work. We spend all of our time and energy nurturing the business relationships that will help us right now, at the expense of the relationships that we developed in past roles, or that may help us in future roles. We never lift our heads long enough to think about the relationships we may need when our current role comes to an end. LinkedIn is the perfect example. How often do you go on LinkedIn, other than when you are looking for a job? When I ask clients how good their LinkedIn profile is, the typical response is something like 'I haven't looked at it in ages, I probably need to do some work on it.' I'm not saying that you need to be spending time on LinkedIn, or social media for that matter! I'm just saying, women in finance often aren't thinking long-term and strategically about their professional relationships.

So how do you work out whom you need to have in your powerbase? I want to keep this quite simple for you. Because I think with a minimal amount of effort, you can quickly identify those people that will have the biggest impact on your career now and in the future. This is my intent in everything I do: to minimise my effort-to-impact ratio. That is, I'm always looking to spend the smallest amount of effort to have the biggest amount of impact.

The roles of the 'powerbase pie'

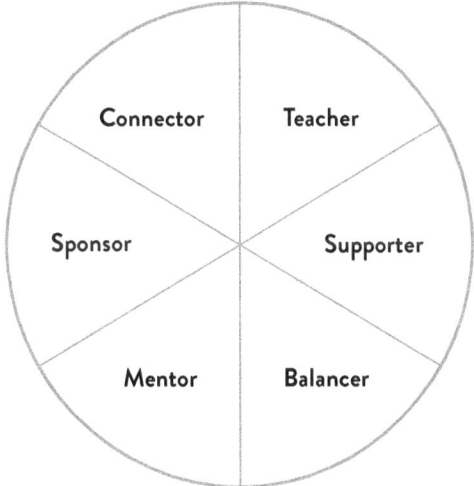

What you're looking for is a group of people to work with you, for you, and on behalf of you, so that it's not all down to you! Let's take a look at the each of the roles you should aim to fill in your powerbase.

Mentor

A mentor is an experienced and trusted adviser, and typically someone who has taken the path you want to take. In effect, they are a role model. Look for someone who has gone through the journey that you want or need to go on, or who demonstrates certain strengths in behaviour, skills, or characteristics that you want to model. Given the context that women in finance operate in, ideally you'd have at least one woman in this segment, but I know this is not always possible or appropriate.

Sponsor

A sponsor is someone that will advocate for you. They will publicly support you and champion you. They are in your corner. Think about this in terms of paying it forward. Whom you have really helped? Is there someone in your organisation who would be less successful without your help, or would have a much more difficult workload? Whose life do you make easier? They are your sponsors.

Connector

A connector is someone who will actively (and ideally, proactively) open up doors for you. Think about people you know who are outstanding at networking. Do you know any salespeople, business partners, or recruiters that could fill this role?

Teacher

A teacher is someone who can teach you what you need to know to get you where you want to be. The teaching may be formal or informal, or ideally a combination of both. Your mentor may be a useful teacher, or you may decide you need a formal, paid teacher or executive coach. Do whatever you have to do to get to where you need to be within the timeframe you want.

Supporter

A supporter is someone who will roll up their sleeves and get their hands dirty to help you achieve something. Supporters will back you when you propose something new. Typically your staff are supporters, and ideally your peers would be as well. That said, think carefully about this one, as people tend to do things for their own reasons, not yours.

Balancer

A balancer is someone who will provide you with comfort if and when you need it. Women in finance are typically strong willed and hold themselves to a very high standard, but this can take a toll on our energy levels, as we're 'always on' – and this is particularly true when we are 'wearing the mask'. We need someone who can see our soft side, a shoulder to lean on (physically or mentally) when we need it. These people are not there to mollycoddle us or indulge us in excuses or bad practices. They are just really good at empathising.

Women in finance need to have people in all pieces of the pie, because the daily grind is hard enough, but, as we've established, your mission is far bigger than that. You are outnumbered and you are operating in a legacy system established by the patriarchy. If you're going to achieve your dream career and live your purpose, you're going to need these people. Ideally, you would have some overlap. You don't want to have so many people in each segment that managing the relationships becomes a full time job on its own! Nor do you want to stretch your relationships so thin that they can't support you in the ways you need.
But on the other end of the spectrum, you don't want to end up with 'key-person dependency', that is, with only one or two people truly in your corner.

A common mistake women in finance make is to expect their boss to fill every one of these roles for them. That's a lot of responsibility to put on someone! It's not an intentional expectation, but something you just sort of assume they should do for you. To be fair, they probably do *try* to do this all for you… but they can't do it all. Not at the level you need them to. Let's be honest, they are finance professionals by trade. Another common mistake women in finance make is to assume that just because you have a great relationship with your boss or particular stakeholders, they will automatically advocate for you and open up doors for you (like Sarah did). Again, they'd probably *like* to do this for you, but realistically they probably won't, because they've got a full workload themselves and furthering your career isn't always going to be front of mind.

That's why this work is so critical. If the people in your world are not clear about where they sit in your powerbase pie, they can't effectively discharge those duties for you. We know that clarity in roles and responsibilities is critical to maximise performance and output. And that's exactly what we're trying to do here. The people in your powerbase need to be clear on what you need from them. Because if they don't know that you see them as a connector, they won't think to open up doors for you. Even if they rant and rave about how good you are, they still might not think to take the next step and say, 'You know what, you should meet Amy. Let me connect you over email when I get back to my desk.'

How to use the powerbase pie

Imagine you are in your perfect job, living your purpose. Close your eyes and visualise yourself in that role. Now ask yourself the following 10 questions, ticking them off as you go:

- ❏ Who are you talking with every day/every week? What level/roles are they in?
- ❏ What 'big meetings' are you presenting at in your role? What level are they at?
- ❏ Who is the most connected person you know? Or best at networking?
- ❏ Whom are you sharing your challenges with?
- ❏ Whom are you going to for support?
- ❏ Whom are you learning from, formally and informally?
- ❏ Who is helping you deliver all the awesome work you're doing?

- Who is helping manage your day?
- How many women are in your pie?
- Who else should be in your powerbase pie?

Draw the powerbase pie at the top of a sheet of paper and write down the people or roles you've identified in the corresponding pie segments.

Now, in a blank space underneath, draw another powerbase pie and ask yourself the same 10 questions about your current role.

You're now ready to reflect on what you've discovered.

- When you look at the two pies side by side, what do you notice? What are the differences?
- Which segments are empty?
- Consider the daily challenges you face at the moment. What roles from the powerbase pie would be helpful in addressing those challenges? Whom do you have in those segments? How effective are they? Do you need to boost that segment?
- Is there anyone whom you spend a considerable amount of time but
  who doesn't sit in any segment? What purpose do they or could they serve for you?
- Are there people in your current world who aren't in your pie but who you wish were?
- How many women are in your pies?

Moving from your current pie to your future pie

We need our powerbase to achieve our goals – to deliver results beyond the numbers. Heck, we need our powerbase to deliver the numbers themselves. But if we are clever about it, we can also use our powerbase to open up doors for us that we didn't think possible. This is critical in such a male-dominated environment – not just for your career, but for all the women who follow.

I can recall situations where senior women in finance have started to leave, and a mere two years later the number of women in leadership roles across finance has more than halved. I'm sure many of us have seen similar situations play out. But imagine if you could have the opposite effect! By reading this book and doing this work, you are giving yourself the opportunity not only to achieve your goals, but to open up doors for the women in finance who come after you – to create a ripple effect that will resonate farther and wider than you can imagine.

6 DO WHAT MATTERS

> 'We need to do a better job of putting ourselves higher on our own to-do list'
>
> *Michelle Obama*

Have you ever attended an awesome workshop or training session and walked away with great notes, great intentions, and great actions that you were 100% convinced would shift the dial for you? You met brilliant people, and promised to connect with them. You were blown away by inspirational speakers whose books you swore you were going to buy. You had a long and inspiring list of podcasts to listen to and socials to follow. And you were so impressed with the stories you heard from other women that you thought, 'You know what? This is possible. I've got the learnings, I've got the contacts, and now all that's left is to implement the actions.'

Then you turned up to work the next day to a bursting calendar and an overflowing email inbox. You have an IBNR analysis to review, clients are
asking for updates and the market has tanked overnight causing a lot of angst on the floor. Very quickly, that list and those actions are filed away with all the other fabulous reference materials you've received over your successful career.

Sound familiar?

What happens in this moment is that we revert to our status quo. Instead of emerging from the training and continuing to build on our learnings, we accidentally slip back into our existing ways of working, perhaps vowing to 'get to that later'. Again and again, we prioritise day-to-day tasks at the expense of our own personal development. We help others to do their jobs but put ourselves, our ambitions, and our aspirations on the backburner.

Let's face it, there's an intrinsic pleasure in helping people. There is no greater satisfaction than helping someone get over the line, working through an issue with a team member, or supporting your boss to give a killer presentation. Helping someone achieve their purpose gets us going. But as the saying goes, we need to put on our own oxygen mask before assisting others. Fit someone else's oxygen mask before your own, and you may not survive to do it again. I think we can all agree that's the opposite of what we want!

In order to thrive and to achieve our vision, we need to learn how to decide what we need to do and where we need to spend our time. But we need to do that while still keeping on top of BAU. And therein lies the issue: we don't know how to do that.

Think back to a time you've been in a meeting when someone has asked for help. You know you don't have time, but you also know that the other people (males!) around the table have their plates full too. Awkwardness ensues, and eventually it's you that offers to help. Now, you may think this has something to do with women being more helpful, more empathetic, or something nice like that. But I'm going to come right out and say that's not it. It's a confidence thing. You didn't have the confidence to just say no. This is the same reason men apply for jobs they are only 70% qualified to do, while women won't even submit their resume until they hit 100%. Without confidence, we struggle to say 'no' even when we know it's not the right thing for us. It is critical that you know how to think and act strategically. You need to know how to put yourself first.

We need to think strategically.

Quite often, when women come to work with me, strategic thinking is high on their list of capabilities to learn and become proficient in. They recognise that this is a critical skill for any senior leader, but particularly for a woman in finance trying to move forward in her career in a way that is congruent with her style and values. One of the things I love about strategic thinking is that it makes time management really easy. So I'm going to cover them in the same chapter.

Think about the journey I mentioned in the introduction to this book. I talked about how women in finance move from the 'learning' phase to the 'growing' phase. It is in the growing phase that you need to learn to shift your focus from operational thinking to strategic thinking. I don't mean strategic in a political sense, which would suggest we were playing a game and manipulating others – that's not my jam. We're thinking strategically about how we're going to achieve our purpose, our dream career, our vision.

Moving from operational to strategic

When you have an *operational* mindset, you think in silos. Audit vs tax, finance vs business, retail vs commercial vs investment. Your thinking about your team and your work is short, narrow, and laser focused. 'What's in it for me' is a common thought process, whether at a conscious or subconscious level. What you think is what you do. So if you're bogged down in the detail, focused on the short-term tasks in front of you, you are smack bang in the middle of *do*er territory. You end up crunched for time because all you're thinking about is getting the 'doer' and 'leader' tasks on your to-do list done – not the best way to do them.

When you have a *strategic* mindset, you think in terms of systems – the 'big picture'. You're thinking at a high level, and possibly longer-term: What are we trying to achieve, how does my team fit into that, and who or what else outside our team should we consider? You're extremely proactive, thinking about the entire network, the 'influence chain', and the matrix of relationships that may be helpful for you. You are open to exploring new ideas and concepts.

When you're thinking about the system, you're more equipped to behave like a true leader. You're out of the weeds – you have your staff doing the doing, so you can take care of more important matters – developing your team, developing your individual staff members, managing relationships, collaborating with peers on better ways of working, remove roadblocks, and escalating potential problems. When you think strategically and lead accordingly, you help the ship sail faster.

As you begin to think more strategically, you will be better able to identify what you need to do to make *your* ship sail faster. I'd like to share with you a practical tool that will help solidify that strategic thinking and apply it to your most helpful tool: your to-do list.

Amplify the impact of your to-do list

Imagine (or pull out if you have it handy) your to-do list. Now, we're going to run each task through two filters.

- Is the task a BAU activity, or a strategic task? A strategic task is one that aligns with your team's strategy or enables you to achieve your vision. BAU is purely operational.
- Is the task low impact or high impact? The best way to think about this is to consider what would happen if you didn't do the task. Would anyone care? Would there be negative consequences for you?

We can envisage these filters as a four-quadrant model:

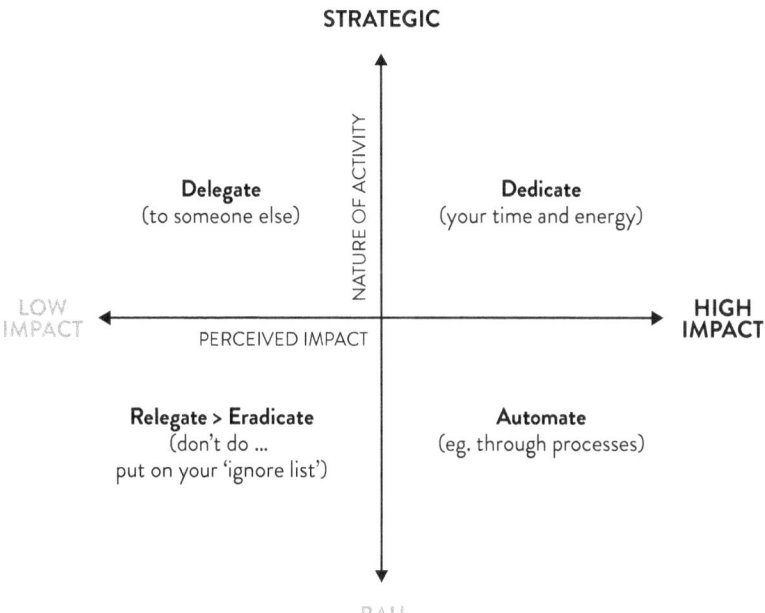

Let's take a closer look at each quadrant, starting with the least important: the low-impact, BAU activities.

Relegate/eradicate

If you have a BAU item on your list and the impact of not doing it is low or negligible (that is, it wouldn't result in a material mistake or regulatory or compliance breach), it probably doesn't deserve your attention. One of my favourite books, *18 Minutes: Find your Focus, Master Distraction, and Get the Right Things Done*[16], by Peter Bregman, provides a daily 18-minute practice to help you perform at your best. What I love most about the book is Bregman's 'ignore list'. In essence, this is the list of 'should-dos' and 'could-dos' that are permanently entrenched in your 'to-do' list. If a task has been on your to-do list for more than three days and still hasn't made it to your calendar, it belongs on your ignore list. Keeping such an item on your to-do list does nothing but serve as a constant reminder of your inability to complete it.

What I love about the ignore list is the intention and the mindset shift that comes with it. By the very act of putting a task on your ignore list, you are saying to yourself, 'I am taking control of my work by choosing to not do this task. And I am confident in doing that, because…' Making the choice to put something on your ignore list immediately empowers you, lightens your mental load, and frees up brain capacity. You do away with unnecessary distractions. You take the stress and guilt of not having completed the task off the table and into the bin. And, perhaps most importantly, you regain a sense of control and confidence in your own decision making.

Automate

In finance, we are highly regulated! We must comply with countless regulations, standards, and guidelines. And even though we may have completely nailed some processes, even though they're repetitive and menial, we still need to do them. Because the impact of not doing them – that is, being subject to a compliance, internal, or external audit – *would* be significant. It would escalate up the chain faster than a possum up a tree! For tasks like this, we need to figure out how to automate them, whether that be through technology (the preferable but possibly expensive or complex option) or through clear manual processes. We need to make carrying out these repetitive, menial tasks as seamless and efficient as possible, so that we can focus on the stuff that matters most.

Delegate

This is where tasks start to become a bit more juicy. These are the tasks that tend to interest us and draw the attention of senior leadership (that is, the people that matter most). But we need to understand that not all strategic tasks are created equal. We need to be discerning about which tasks we need to do ourselves, and which ones we can oversee and supervise. Because if we do all the detailed tasks associated with strategic activity ourselves, we're straight back into 'doing-land'. I understand that certain sensitive or commercially confidential tasks will require your personal attention, and that's fine – but for the most part this is not the best use of your time. The ability to delegate low-impact strategic items not only frees up your time, it also gives your staff a great opportunity to get involved in the strategic work (which I'm sure is something you've been asked before).

Dedicate

Now we're striking gold! This is where the action happens. Activities that are both high impact and strategic in nature are the ones you should be dedicating the most time and energy to. These are the activities that will bring you closer to your vision as well as helping you continue to succeed where you are right now. These are also the activities that, when done well, will raise your profile within your organisation and help you develop new leadership skills. This is where you want to play!

This quadrant should include any items that involve the CEO/MD or other senior executives. In particular, you should dedicate special attention to work that involves multiple executives across the organisation with an interest in the activity. You should be able to align such work with one of your organisation's strategic objectives – to be able to say, 'Once completed, this work will contribute to the achievement of X objective in our 2020 strategy.' This is your opportunity to really go big in your organisation! Ideally, your role within the activity would include interaction with one or more of these executives, but at the very least you should ensure that someone in your powerbase will acknowledge your contribution to those executives. Completing tasks in this quadrant gives you an opportunity to learn or practise some of the capabilities or ways of working that you have identified in your vision. Perhaps they contribute to 'your edge'.

You will find that the energy associated with these activities is high. When you see the opportunities that sit within the task or project, it revs you up. However, because a focus on this type of activities is new to you, there are a few things that may trip you up:

- Strategic activities often have a longer lead time that is variable. When we are trying to figure out what activity to do, we are likely to do the one that has the hard, imminent deadline because we perceive we have flexibility in the strategic one.

- Working on strategic activities often requires thinking and planning time – two luxuries we're really not used to affording ourselves during business hours! After spending most of your career reacting and responding to issues, the idea of sitting at your desk to really think something through might feel indulgent or inappropriate. It's just not our natural working style.

- These activities can't be done alone! They will force you to engage with your powerbase. In fact, they are the perfect excuse to engage with the people you want in your powerbase.

The great thing about using filters like this is that once you get this right – once you can clearly identify which tasks you should dedicate your time and energy to, and which you should automate, delegate, or ignore – everything else just falls into place. You develop your team, you create efficient processes, and you set up a system whereby you and your team do only valued activities with a tangible impact. Instead of balancing endless spinning plates on your hands, your feet, your chin, and your head (you know what I'm talking about!), you can throw the plates to the people or places that make sense until you're left spinning only those plates that fulfil your aspirations.

So why did I share that with you? Because we're deep in the 'bringing your purpose to life' phase now, and it's time to get practical. I don't want to hear you say, 'I can't find the time to do this and I'm miserable.' I don't want you to tell me, 'I'm not getting the results I want.' I want to help you take control of your career and be the change you want to see for women in finance. I want to give you the strategies, tactics, and practical actions to execute on your purpose right here, right now.

But just reading this book isn't enough. Carving your own path takes deep commitment to yourself. Only you know your time, only you know your vision, and only you can make the right choices for you. There's a saying, 'If you don't choose your future, someone else will.' And how scary is that!

I want to wrap up this chapter by sharing two incredibly powerful phrases that I'd love you to learn and use:

- "Yes, and…"
- "Yes, but…"

We don't like to say no. So we say yes… to everything! Even if it doesn't serve us and help move our ship forward. It's an inner block, a subconscious fear of how saying no might be perceived. That fear will start to erode as you become more confident, but until then, I want to arm you with the tools to overcome it.

When you are asked something and you wish you could just say no, I'd like you to use one of the above phrases instead. Here are some examples:

- 'Yes, (I'd be happy to,) and I can get it to you in two weeks, after I've finished the task I'm working on.'
- 'Yes, (I'd be happy to,) but first I need you to meet with Peter and collect information to inform our conversation.'
- 'Yes, (I can meet that crazy deadline,) and let's talk about the scope of the work so we can make it fit within your timing.'
- 'Yes, (I could do that,) but actually I feel like that task should probably sit with John.'

What's really handy about the phrases above is that they will never burn bridges or erode relationships. Said with the right tone, and in the right spirit of strategically putting the relationship above the work itself, these phrases can create better results for all parties. Win/win. Try it out.

Do the strategic thinking, identify what will serve you and amplify your impact at work, and change the way you respond to requests accordingly. You are not expected to unflinchingly, unconditionally say yes to everything. You might think you are, but you're not. Remember, you're not a servant. Do the high impact work that you deserve to be doing. Put your own oxygen mask on first.

6.1 META ACTIVITY 2: INTEGRATE YOUR PURPOSE

By now you should be able to tick off that you:

- ❏ Know what revs you up
- ❏ Understand the mindset you need to deal with uncertainty
- ❏ Know what you need to do to become change confident and remove your mask
- ❏ Know your purpose
- ❏ Understand that being proactive is the strategic advantage you need to bring your vision to life and amplify your impact at work
- ❏ Know who is in your powerbase and whom you need in your powerbase to achieve your vision
- ❏ Understand that having a lens of 'value' will free up the time (and headspace) to enable you to focus on the strategic activities required to amplify your impact and achieve your vision.

I'm really excited to share this next meta activity with you. This model explains how you incorporate your purpose and new skills into your current job – exactly where you're at. The resource I'm about to share with you will allow you to act on and implement all the information you now know about yourself, and all the additional capabilities you now have access to, so that you can

(a) perform more effectively at work *now* – and have people notice it – and (b) practise the mindset, behaviours, and skills that you will need in your dream job.

This resource will allow you to implement any new behaviour, mindset, or skill into your work right now. I use this process in literally all my coaching, facilitation and training programs – it's that good! You're about to learn, in detail, how you can solve current and immediate business problems while at the same time building the capability, behaviours, and attributes you need to achieve your purpose.

It is so critical that any change we make is real, achievable, and impactful.

To put it another way, every goal should be 'possible in its context', 'probable in its achievement', and 'powerful in its resulting impact'.

If we want to progress from Point B straight to Point D on the journey model, and bypass C altogether, we need change to be possible and real. When change is real, we can see it and we can do it. One of the biggest challenges when you find your purpose is figuring out how to practically apply it in your current context. We often find our purpose only to wonder, *What now?* To make the change 'real', we need to look at our work week as five whole days full of opportunities to create changes that will bring our purpose to life. We also need to break down our purpose into chunks of activity that we can implement within those days.

You know your mindset change is real when you start to notice a shift in your reactions to circumstances. When you start to focus on creating opportunities rather than dwelling on consequences. When you find perspective on issues that previously would have sent you into a tailspin. When you shrug your shoulders, say 'no big deal', and move on to considering how you can improve next time instead of spending the rest of the day beating yourself up.

You know behaviour change is real when others notice a difference in the way you behave and communicate with them. When you are sought out for advice *before* transactions are dealt, instead of at the 11th hour when the contract is just about to be signed. When you are asked to attend meetings that are usually only for the 'inner circle'. When your peers come to you for advice.

If you believe you have implemented change, yet nothing in your world is changing – work continues to be a struggle and you're not getting the results you want – then the change isn't real. The change isn't possible in the way that you have defined it or executed it. If you find yourself in this situation, it's time to get honest with yourself about the context you are operating in, the outcome you are aiming for and the actions you are taking.

For example, if you decide to deliver insight (connected to your purpose) on an area that your organisation doesn't care about (disconnected to context), there won't be real change. You might notice a difference, but if the organisation doesn't care about it, it's as if it doesn't exist. No one will say anything different about you, and it won't lead to new growth or development opportunities.

Change is hard.

And it's especially hard when you're in a minority group like women in finance. So we need to make the process of implementing change as easy as possible. By easy, I mean actually doable – achievable, practical. There's no point signing up for a marathon in two weeks' time if you can't run a kilometre now. You might have some extra-hard changes in mind that you want to create, like developing a flexible way of working that really works for you. But changes like this will never happen unless you make them easy to do and easy to follow.

There are many things that can get in the way of creating change. Time gets in the way all the time, leading us to feel that it's 'better the devil you know than the devil you don't'. Too many options create paralysis by analysis. We run short of perseverance and resilience – change might seem like a great idea at the time, and you might be thrilled to get involved with some massive action at first… but what happens when you get to next week, or next month, and you still haven't hit your goal? Rome wasn't built in a day.

All the above reasons contribute to why organisations are typically so slow when it comes to proactive change. It's not for lack of want or even understanding of need. Sometimes it's just too hard! So to implement change effectively, we need to make it *easy*. It's a little like committing to a diet: you know it's easy to eat healthy if you never bring unhealthy food into the house. So you start by creating those conditions. You plan your meals, write a shopping list, shop online to avoid being tempted and making impulse buys… you get my drift. We need to make it easy.

When you try something new, your brain immediately seeks feedback on that experience. Is this something we want to do again, or something we don't want to do again? So whenever we do something new, we want to stack the decks in favour of a positive outcome so that we can trigger the reward function in our brain and be naturally encouraged to repeat that behaviour. Upon repetition, this 'new' behaviour mindset or activity becomes habit – the way we naturally work, without even thinking.

As well as making the changes we implement as easy as possible, we need to make sure that they actually deliver results – that they are impactful. There are a couple of reasons for this. First of all, you have a job to do! You need to continue to kick ass in your current job, while also working towards the greater vision you've now set for yourself. I have promised you throughout the book that you will be able to execute your purpose exactly where you're at, and you will – but only if the changes you make are impactful. The second benefit of impactful work is that it elevates your performance. When you increase the impact of your work, people will notice that shift – both in the results you're achieving and in the way you're achieving them. This will open up new opportunities organically (or through a bit of influence!) in your current position. You'll start to feel 'mobilised' and you will notice very quickly that you are being given bigger and better opportunities.

We now know what we're aiming for: change that's real, doable, and delivers results. The question is, how do we get there?

We get there through the intersection of three factors:

- Context: the context of our role in the workplace

- Clarity: a detailed vision of what we want and where we want to get to

- Connection: connecting change to something we already do or utilising the connections we have created through our powerbase.

When you have context and clarity, it's real. You know what's really going on and you know what you're doing. When you have clarity and connection, it's easy. You know what you're doing, and you have the networks to do it. When you have connection and context, it's impactful. You have networks to make change happen, and you know what's really going on.

When all three factors intersect, you have everything you need to implement behaviour change that will create growth and help you achieve your vision.

Context

Context is everything. Consider how wide the gap can be between learning in a training room and applying that learning at work. In a simulated environment such as a training room, we can get really caught up with a change, thinking, 'yes, yes, yes!' But then you get back to 'the real world', and your learning suddenly feels so distant and impossible that you don't even consider applying it.

Whenever you're considering how you might apply something new, ask yourself: What's *really* going on? What is the *real* context you are operating in? Not the exaggerated context you whinge to your friends about, not the glorified context you might wish you were in, but the real, objective context.

This can be hard, because if your context is challenging you at the moment (you don't fit in, you're not getting opportunities, you don't feel valued, etc), your perspective can be tainted. So you need to put on your perspecticles! A useful way of doing this is to consider how an outsider would describe your context if they were to look in on you and share their observations. For example: you are a senior woman in finance, with a certain level of influence and authority that comes with the role and years of experience, you are well respected by others, and people are willing to do work for you. These are objective observations.

Once you have an objective view of your context, consider what elements of your purpose you can bring to life right now. Maybe you can create improvement, or break down silos, or open up relationships outside your function. It can be anything. The important thing is to be clear on what you're going to do and what that will look like – in detail.

Now, the question becomes: *How* or *where* can we apply that component of our purpose in our current context? Now, we must find – or better still, create – an opportunity to bring that component of our purpose to life now. That is how we make change possible in the real world.

Clarity

Reaching clarity about the change you want to create is the first part of making it easy. It is also the area I find my clients struggle with the most. Women in finance give their all at work, focusing solely on their current workload, at their current organisation, in their current reality, at the exclusion of all else. Clarity is about knowing *exactly* where you want to go, and this requires vision, strategic thinking, and focus on possibility and opportunity. Clarity is about characterising your goal at the deepest level of detail: what it looks like, what it feels like, the change or difference it will bring to your life. This kind of granular detail is the key to knowing where you want to go.

If I had a dollar for every time a client has told me they want something, but been unable to describe to me this elusive 'something' in any kind of detail! What we see, we do. So if we cannot see the change we want in our mind's eye, we have no hope in bringing it to life. Being able to clearly visualise the change you want to see is a key part of making it easy to achieve. It is a necessary step before you can identify the new behaviours or activities required to implement that change.

Connection

Connection is the second part of the impact equation. When you connect with the right people in your workplace, and recognise the connection between your purpose and your work, you can choose to make the incremental changes that will really make a difference. This is where the magic happens! An evolution takes place as your context shifts and your capability – demonstrated through your connected actions – grows. Every time you undertake a new action that you have connected to an existing activity or engage with one of your new connections, you are levelling up your capability. You are actively demonstrating that you do more now than you did before. And because you're doing it in a real-world context, it's making a real-world impact. People are noticing. And they're starting to comment: 'Rachael is doing well these days! Boy, she has really lifted. Perhaps we should get her involved with the new project we've got coming up?' New capability, new context, new opportunity. And so the cycle continues. It's awesome.

Connection is also about being able to connect the 'new stuff' to activities you already do. The 'if-then' strategy, more formally known as the setting of 'implementation intentions[17]' (a term coined by psychologist Peter Gollwitzer), basically entails adding a new action to an action we already take. This popular approach to habit creation makes things much easier by taking the thought work out of doing something new. Not only does it help us overcome the mental barrier and begin to reinforce this new neural pathway in our brain, it also ensures that what we are learning and doing will contribute to our existing performance/activities in some way.

For example, in Chapter 6: Do what matters, we talked about reallocating items on our to-do list in order to make sure we're investing our energy and effort into tasks that are strategic and high impact. If the change you want to make is to incorporate this model into your current job, you would create the following 'if-then' rule for yourself: *If* you are about to put something on your to-do list, *then* before you do so, run the task through the model in Chapter 6. That way, only those tasks that are strategic and high impact will make it onto your to-do list. Do this enough, and you will reinforce that neural pathway to the point that this thought process happens automatically for any new task. Once the pathways are embedded, like a well-trodden path in the bush, the new actions become easy to do.

How about an example?

Let's say you're working on a big project (*context*). You've identified that one of the stakeholders on the project – an executive from an external business unit – is someone that you want in your powerbase (*clarity*). From the work you've already done, you realise they could be important in achieving your vision. They could open up doors outside of your direct team, which, given that you can't see much room to move upwards in your own department within the next couple of years, might be the move you need in order to continue to progress towards your vision. Add to that the simple fact that having another advocate in your corner at that level is critical, and this project starts to seem like a great way in (*context*).

Now something comes up that requires input from that stakeholder (*connection*). Usually someone else on the project would liaise with them, but it seems like this could be a great opportunity for you. Having realised that they are important to your world, you decide to meet them directly. It seems like the additional time investment would be worth it. And as an added benefit, you'll obtain the information directly from them rather than introducing a middle-man into the process, which you can see is more efficient (*connection*).

Let me give you another example. You need to prepare a presentation to the Board (*context*). While the topic you are presenting on is clear, you know there's related work happening elsewhere in the business. You realise that this is an opportunity to (a) proactively meet a potential powerbase person from that part of the business, and (b) demonstrate your strategic thinking by engaging with them proactively and incorporating that thinking into your presentation (*clarity*). You believe that if you do these things, not only will your presentation have greater impact, but you're more likely to get an 'easy yes' for your work (*connection*).

I hope that these examples and the work we've done so far help you to clearly see how you can apply your learning in the 'real' context.

Here are the key questions to ask yourself:

Context

- What is going on?
- What is *really* going on? What are your preconceived ideas about the work/people/area? What organisational sensitivities are at play?
- What are you working on?

You will get to the bottom of these questions by taking a proactive approach, using systems thinking, and adopting a change-confident mindset. (Refer back to Chapter 2: Take off your mask.)

Clarity

- Ideally, what do you want?
- What would it look like/what would happen if you were achieving your vision?
- What does it look like when you are doing the activities associated with your vision?

Source this information through awareness of your motivators and your purpose, and break it down into shorter, more tangible milestones. (Refer back to Chapter 1: Light up your motivators.)

Connection

- How will you incorporate any additional steps you need to take? What 'if-then' strategies will you create?
- What is the timeline of those steps, and how will you use your calendar to facilitate this?
- Whom in your powerbase will you engage?

Source this information from the actions you have identified so far through this book and your key powerbase people. (Refer back to

Meta Activity 1: Connect to your purpose and Chapter 5: Establish your powerbase.)

Although we're only two sections in, I'm sharing this with you now because we've covered an awful lot that you can start to implement for greater impact already. You can already get rid of that 'meh' feeling and approach your work with greater purpose and fulfillment from this moment on.

By doing the work to make changes today that are real, easy, and impactful, you will also be implementing skills that will directly help you do your existing job better. You will overcome your current challenges and achieve your current performance goals with greater confidence, knowing that the effort is worth it because it aligns and contributes to your bigger purpose.

You now have a proven process that you can use every time you want to implement a new skill or capability: know your context, be clear on what the change is, and connect the actions associated with the change to actions you already do. In the next section, you will learn a huge amount on how to really bring all of this learning to the forefront, but I want you to know that you can start *now*. You are no longer a victim of your context.

PART 3:
APPROACH

7 PRESENT WITH CONFIDENCE

"The way you overcome shyness is to become so wrapped up in something that you forget to be afraid."

Lady Bird Johnson

'I need to improve my presentation skills.' If I had a dollar for every time a woman in finance said this to me! Usually what they really mean is 'I don't like to present.' In the corporate landscape, being able to present well is an essential skill. Many women are acutely aware of the increasing pressure to present as they move into more senior leadership roles, and it can lead to serious anxiety. An aversion to presenting can feed existing confidence issues, which then adds to the stress, which negatively impacts performance… it quickly becomes a vicious cycle.

But *why* don't we like to present? Let's be honest, traders aside, us finance folk aren't natural sales people. Even though it's now part of my job to stand up and talk in front of hundreds of people, I grew up being the kid standing behind the showman (both my best friend and my sister were happy playing that role!). For most of my life, my preference has been to work backstage – on the lights, on the curtains, or in the orchestra away from the stage. Maybe we're just generally quiet or shy, and being in front of people has never been our strong suit. Or maybe we've stuffed up a few presentations in the past (and of course, they're the only ones you remember!). Alternatively, you might not have much experience in giving presentations at all. It's perfectly natural to feel nervous about doing something you've never done before. Women in particular have a tendency to assume that we need to be an expert at something before we do it. And we apply this assumption not just to the act of presenting, but also to the technicalities of whatever it is we're presenting on. We feel that we must be an expert not only on presenting, but also on the subject matter itself.

Have you ever taken an extended period of leave, only to feel a little awkward and out of place when you get back? As everyone rushes from meeting to meeting, busying themselves with important tasks, it's easy to feel out of the loop. Often, the longer you've been away, the more uncomfortable you feel. After taking a sabbatical, long service leave, or maternity leave, you might feel that you missed out on too much while you were away, that you've been 'out of the game for too long'. It might feel almost like starting again, as if you need to re-earn people's respect and re-establish your credibility. Whether you know it or not, this thinking erodes your confidence.

I think we experience a very similar mental process when we think about presenting. We focus on our lack of experience, or mistakes we've made in the past, or the negative ways people might perceive us, instead of simply applying ourselves to the task at hand. So while I agree that there are some elements of 'presentation skills' that need to be taught, I actually think the root cause of the problem has nothing to do with presenting. It's about confidence, it's about conviction, and, ultimately, it's about purpose. If you know *why* you're presenting, it's far easier to do.

I want to share with you a different way of looking at delivering a presentation that I hope will create a shift in your mindset (and ultimately confidence) about your ability to deliver a kickass presentation. But this new approach is applicable well beyond presentations. I am about to share with you one of the most important leadership capabilities around communication.

Before we jump into this concept, let me pose a question:

Is communication about results or relationships?

Many would say that communication is about delivering results, because ultimately that's what we're here for at work. But there's a second school of thought that says communication is all about relationships, and if we do relationships right, the results will come. I personally think there's a lot of sense in that – but try telling it to someone facing a massive deadline!

Our challenge with communication is to balance results and relationships

I've said earlier that relationships are a key currency for leadership today, and that's true. However, if we focus too much on relationships, we inadvertently waste time, we give in too easily (remember the distinction we made between being in service and being a servant?), and ultimately, we don't deliver. A focus on relationships at the exclusion of all else is an inefficient way to achieve business results.

So what if we focus on results instead? We do presentations to get results, right? We present strategies and annual results so that we can improve our business processes. We present to investors so that they will choose to invest with our organization. We present at company town hall meetings so that our employees are informed and feel included.

Sure enough, the way most companies approach presentations *does* reflect an exclusive focus on results. Finance presentations are typically a one-way transmission of information. And they are boring (I'm sorry, but let's be honest!). They usually run according to the same tired old formula: introduction, work performed, conclusion, Q&A. Even the Q&A is tightly controlled and highly scripted. This approach can deliver results, but it does nothing for our relationships.

How then, do we reach a balance between results and relationships? We do it with *facilitation*. Facilitation is the intersection between conversation and presentation. It is a way of sharing information that encourages collaboration and contribution, and delivers results and outcomes. Facilitation means literally facilitating a conversation among the people in the room in order to achieve a specific outcome, within a specific time period. Being a facilitator is a little like being an air-traffic controller – coordinating everything for the planes, but not actually flying them. Moving people toward a desired outcome in this way is an unbeatable strategy for moving things forward.

Facilitation is not only what happens when we balance results and relationships. It's where we use relationships to *enhance* our results.

We do not have to be a professional facilitator to facilitate…. and I would say that every leader today *must* be able to facilitate. If we want to leverage the best minds in the organisation and get the best results, we must facilitate conversation and resolution of issues, whether that be with your team, your peers, the Board, the business, your clients, your investors, or your market. Facilitation is a leadership imperative.

Presentation vs facilitation

Traditional presentations are about one-way sharing of information and answering of questions. The inherent assumption in this is that the presenter is the fount of all knowledge and must be able to answer every possible question thrown their way. It's only natural that we would feel fearful of being put in a position where we might be 'shown up' as not knowing everything. The supposition of ultimate knowledge is ridiculous, but it's not so far removed from the pressure we've been putting on ourselves every day of our careers. We're expected to uphold the highest standard of accuracy and knowledge, and we hold ourselves to that standard in every task we do. But this perfection mentality is never more active than when we are asked to give a presentation. And, understandably, it freaks us out.

When you are facilitating, you are not there to give all the answers. You are there to ask the questions and hold the space so that a particular outcome is achieved. In fact, the word *facilitate* is derived from the Latin *facile*, 'easy to do'. Your role as facilitator, then, is to make achieving an outcome easy to do. It is certainly not to solve the problem or answer the question yourself. Facilitation is also a great opportunity to showcase your ability to think and act strategically, which is a concept we covered in Chapter 4: Own your impact. Prepare for this by doing the systems thinking relevant to your meeting: what are the other people, processes and systems that may contribute to or be dependent on the topic you are facilitating.

So I've lightened the burden a bit here. Great! But you're probably still not sure how much you'd enjoy speaking in front of a group of senior businessmen or at a big company town hall meeting!

So let's now revisit a concept I shared earlier in this book: that of being 'in service'. Being in service means having the mindset, attitudes, and actions to help others. It is not about you; it is all about them. Not pandering to them, of course, but focusing your energy and effort on serving them. This is the mindset that will forever change how you think about facilitating in meetings and on stage.

Be clear on three things:

- What do they want? What do they not have that they can get from you? What makes it worth it for them to give up their time to listen to you speak?

- Why you are the right person to give it to them? What have you done or what do you do that puts you in the best position to facilitate this meeting?

- What is your intent? If you go into a meeting with an intent of generosity or curiosity, that will show. Even if you stuff up, if you are clear on your intent and your intent is worthy, they will go easy on you.

Matt Church is one of the nation's best keynote speakers, and I've had the privilege of having him mentor me in the art of speaking and thought leadership. He has a saying: 'State over script.' What he means by that is that what you say is less important than how you say it. What is the energy that you bring to it? What is your intent? Church's position is that your state will trump your script every time.

'That's not true!' I hear you scream! 'We need to be accurate, otherwise we get cut down!'

I hear you, and I get it. But I also believe that Matt is right, so I want to get really practical on how you can prepare to facilitate an outstanding meeting in a way that will help you develop your state as much as your script. These are the *four Ps of presentation through facilitation*, and they are the key to releasing the pressure valve and being more confident in your presentations.

The four Ps ('4Ps') of presentation through facilitation

PURPOSE	PEOPLE
• What is the purpose of the meeting? • What is the desired outcome of the meeting? • What is the context that surrounds the purpose and outcome? • What is the role of data/numbers?	• Who is your audience? • What is going on in their world? 　– What are their needs and aspirations? 　– What are their frustrations and distractions? 　– What are they hearing and seeing from others in the organisation or industry? 　– What else do you know about them that would be useful to consider before your meeting? • How will you engage them in the conversation during the meeting?
PROCESS	PRACTICE
• What information do you need? • Who can provide you with this information? • What is the process for acquiring that information within an appropriate timeline?	• When will you prepare? • Who will you get to review your content (and possibly even watch you practice)? • What else do you need to know about the room you'll be in and the technology you'll be using in order to ensure an effective meeting?

Dealing with data

One of the common challenges faced by Finance is that no one cares about the numbers as much as they do. As a result, finance folk are often criticised for talking about the wrong data in the wrong way. Data destroys the conversation, eroding the business partner or client relationship that follows. However, if we reframe data from being just the cold hard facts, to a strong facilitation tool, we'll find it's possible to bring people onside with the numbers.

Data can also be used as a facilitation tool to:

- Discover commonalities to bring groups of people together
- Leverage strengths by identifying where they lie
- Break down biases by widening perspectives
- Desensitize emotional topics by focusing energy on solutions[18]

Using data effectively goes a long way to helping the finance conversation and this directly aligns with our 4Ps of presentation through facilitation.

However, here is the most important thing about including data and facts in your presentations: you must have a story to tell. Because without a relevant story, the numbers are useless. And to bust further finance misconceptions, when you are presenting to people outside of finance, the story isn't the numbers. It's words. It's insight. It's describing the business' strategy and focus and how that translates into drivers of performance. Only then do you describe how that is reflected in the numbers, and most importantly, the relevance (the 'so what') of that information for now and in the future.

The great thing about stories, is that people remember them. Understanding this intersection between numbers and words is what will make your presentations count.

> I worked with a financial services leader who was in charge of leading a system implementation within her organisation. She is dyslexic, and held the belief that this was a contributing factor to her not being a strong presenter. We focused an entire session on preparing the 4 Ps and the feedback she received from that presentation was that she nailed it. However, it wasn't as much about the presentation of the content itself than around the preparation she undertook after our session. By covering off on each step in the 4Ps process, she had engaged her C-suite stakeholders, she understood the context, and she could connect the dots between the work she was presenting, what each stakeholder in the room cared about and the strategic objective of the project itself in the context of the organisation. This took the pressure off her and she found the presentation easy.

The key is to detach from the outcome itself and focus on the process you need to work through to get there. The questions contained in the 4Ps might seem like a lot, and if you haven't got much experience facilitating meetings they may take a bit of getting used to. But with practice, this process will become second nature and the questions above will simply serve as a reminder checklist.

A note about time

One of the common misconceptions my clients have is that all of this preparation work needs to happen outside of core work hours. That this isn't 'real work', it's just 'nice to have'. This couldn't be further from the truth. Cast your mind back to the work we did around determining how strategic and impactful tasks are. In most instances, facilitating a meeting will be both, and will fall into the 'Dedicate' quadrant. So it's absolutely imperative that you give this preparation work the time and energy that it deserves. The way you facilitate and ask questions in meetings will determine the way people perceive and remember you. And that can be a game changer in your career.

Do you remember when Prince Harry and Meghan Markle came to Australia? You may have seen the cute photo outside the opera house that was shared on Twitter. All the chairs are out, and Prince Harry is on stage practising to a lone Meghan. I reckon if preparation is important enough for a prince, it's important enough for a woman in finance!

When we present in a productive way – when we bring a group together to engage in active problem solving – we deliver results. The great thing about this new approach to presenting is that it gives you a little boost of confidence – and that might be all you need to get started. From here, the more you do it, the more your confidence will grow. Each time you present confidently, those neural pathways will be reinforced, until confidence becomes a natural, automatic part of presenting. The day will come when the anxiety you once felt is a distant memory.

8 COMMUNICATE FOR INFLUENCE

"How wonderful it is that nobody need wait a single moment before starting to improve the world."

Anne Frank

'Wow, that didn't go as I expected!'

Have you ever had that thought as you've walked out of a meeting? I can tell you exactly what went wrong here: your intent did not equal your impact.

It's easy to justify to yourself why a meeting went a little pear shaped. It's easy to say, 'They missed the point, they went in with their agenda and wouldn't let it go, they weren't ready to hear what we had to say.' And those things may even be true… to an extent. But let me remind you of something: We must take 100% responsibility for our impact. So even if all of those justifications are true, you must still take ownership for that: 'I didn't communicate the point clearly, I didn't give them a reason to let go of their agenda, I didn't deal with an underlying problem that stopped them being ready to listen.'

If your message doesn't land with your audience the way you intended, *you* have to own that. That doesn't mean you should beat yourself up, though. Actually, taking 100% responsibility is very empowering, as it means we have the ability to influence the outcome. It's about following every reason, justification, or complaint with 'What could I have done differently to have the impact I desired?'

Let's face it: in the world of finance, communication is not usually people's strong suit. Yes, it's a stereotype, but people in finance communicate primarily using facts, data, and logic. They are often fairly 'straighty 180' and don't like to engage in esoteric or 'what if' conversations (or use of terms like 'straighty 180'!). Ask anyone outside of finance and they'll probably agree that conversations with finance people are generally not the most scintillating of the week. These bleak facts give women in finance a great opportuntity to lead the way in communicating with impact – however, we must balance that opportunity with the responsibility of creating the impact we want.

We need to communicate for impact, not information

What I mean by that is we need to be proactive about our communication. We need to be strategic and tactical about who we communicate with, the words we use, and the timing we choose. You're probably starting to feel like communication is the cornerstone of every strategy in this book! And in some ways, it is. We communicate with our body, our face, our words, our limbs, and our tone; in what we write and also in what we say. Communication and behaviour are, in a sense, one and the same. And the way we communicate is an essential element of our leadership identity.

What that means is that every time we reach a new level of performance and leadership, our communication also needs to level up. To put this in the context of the four stages I introduced at the start of the book, you would expect your communication in Stage 1, 'learning', to be quite different to your communication in Stage 2, 'growing', and different again in Stage 3, 'thriving'. This doesn't mean that when you're 'thriving' your language becomes so jargon-y and vanilla that no one quite understands what you're saying! It simply means that your language changes as you adapt to your new situation and the different impact you need to make at each stage of your career. To continue to succeed as you move through the levels, you must be proactive in the way you communicate.

Appreciate and adapt to diverse communication styles

As I mentioned in Chapter 1, one of the most valuable takeaways from our work on subconscious motivators is a much clearer picture of how we are perceived. This gives us the opportunity to reflect on whether that perception matches with our self-identity and the way we want to be perceived. Further to that, as we start to get practical about it, we can drill down and identify the behaviours and nuances of our communication style that may contribute to that perception. This is highly valuable information when it comes to communicating for impact.

Let me give you an example that may feel familiar.

Imagine you've just completed an in-depth analysis on a certain financial instrument, market movement, or accounting standard. You schedule time with your boss to take them through it, and at the end of the meeting (which you think has gone very well, by the way), they say, 'Great, thanks for that. Could you please email it through to me and I'll send back any comments.' You can't help but think, 'Why? The memo doesn't have any additional information outside what I've shared already. What's the point? Have I just wasted the past half hour?' It's intensely frustrating to feel like you've just given it all in a meeting, only to discover that it didn't give you the approval you were hoping for.

Your mind can go all sorts of places from here. You can quickly spiral from frustration, to resentment, and even to fear, depending on your circumstances. But you know what? It may simply be that your boss' preferred communication style is different from yours. You may prefer to do things in meetings or conversations, where you can see the person you're talking to, gauge their body language, and inject personality and emphasis into your dialogue. But they may prefer to read that same information in silence, where they can process it at their own pace, reflect, and hum and ha in their own space. In this example, if the impact you wanted was to receive approval on your analysis, it may have been more effective to adapt to your boss' communication preference in the first place.

There are many ways to categorise people's communication preferences, and when we're using communication for impact, it's about how we can communicate to most effectively get our point across. Our role as a communicator is to help our audience understand. iWAM uses communication preferences of reading, listening, doing, and seeing. The commonly used VAK model uses similar categories, but different terminology – Visual corresponds to seeing, Auditory to listening, and Kinaesthetic to doing. Regardless of the terminology you use, what you need to be asking yourself is: How does your audience prefer to receive information? You might be able to make an educated guess based on your past experience with them. If you haven't worked with them much, or not in a way that helps you answer this question, find out who would know this and talk with them.

Communication: What's the point?

We need to be clear about the impact we want from our communication. The impact is going to differ depending on the context, the relationship, the topic, and the time. Here are just a few common desired impacts for women in finance:

- *To engage*: We may need to engage our team or stakeholders in an idea, an analysis, or a change. We may need to communicate purely to engage our audience – to get them 'on board'. A common mistake among women in finance is to assume that communication for engagement's sake (i.e. engagement being an outcome) isn't a thing. It is a very important thing, especially if we need to take people 'on a journey'.

- *To move from rapport to relationship*: When we are establishing our future powerbase, we need to deepen some relationships. Think about how you engaged with the CEO or MD as you worked your way up the organisational ladder. At first, you may have simply smiled and said a polite 'hello' as you passed them in the hallway. As you progressed, you may have had to present information to them and had something of a dialogue (or maybe it was more of a monologue!). As the dialogue with your CEO (or whoever it might be) starts to open, in order to really open up the lines of communication, your relationship needs to change, and you can effect that change through the way you communicate.

- *To provide clarity*: Sometimes communication is not to share new information, but to provide clarity or certainty around information that has previously been shared. This happens frequently if you are a finance business partner or auditor! The impact of clarity cannot be underestimated. Uncertainty and lack of clarity reduce productivity and effectiveness in the workplace. If you want your team to produce quality work in an efficient manner, you need to provide clarity.

- *To achieve a particular result or outcome*: Sometimes we just need to deliver. And that is okay. But don't let this be your default! It's all too easy to undervalue the power of relationships in our organisations, assuming there is an expectation and bias for facts and data. We tend to focus instead on results, which can come across as a bit one-dimensional, or even as a blunt stick, at times.

The relationship between impact and influence

We know that influence is an important leadership capability. Quite often the impact we want to have through our conversations and behaviours is to influence an outcome. This is particularly the case for women in finance, because they are so underrepresented in leadership roles. The male-dominated industry of finance has, over time, led to a 'system' of unconscious bias that sits beneath the culture of the industry. It is inherent in almost everything you do.

I've had conversations with clients about potential turnover within their team where I've had to point out that if the turnover happens as they expect, there will be no women left in the team. Quite often clients have been left dumbfounded by this observation, honestly admitting that it hadn't even crossed their mind – they hadn't even looked at gender bias or differences within the team. I'd like to be really clear here that these are great, well-meaning clients. They treat their people really well. But they have a blind spot – and they're not alone. Many finance leaders (and other execs, to be fair) neglect to even consider gender bias or diversity in their organisation on a day to day basis.

What this means is that the influence of women in finance needs to be second to none.

In order to really nail influence, you need three things:

- A powerbase of strong relationships
- Exceptional communication skills: presentation, facilitation, collaboration
- A proactive mindset

Luckily for you, these are all things we've covered in this book. So you've got the tools you need.

When you have these three elements, your ability to influence increases significantly as you:

- Mobilise, amplify, and leverage your impact through your relationships
- Perform with confidence and believe in what you're trying to achieve (If you don't believe it, you don't have a hope in hell of influencing others! So this one is key.)
- Operate with an executive presence that makes people stop, listen, and want to act.

If you do can do this effectively, your career trajectory will go to plan. You will be able to create the conditions you need to perform with purpose exactly where you're at.

Communicate for impact: 7-step approach

STEP 1: Set a clear goal.

This seems so basic, but that's why so many people overlook it. You need to set a goal for the meeting based on the impact you want to have. That goal should be SMART: Specific, Measurable, Achievable, Realistic, and Time bound. A fuzzy goal like 'I want you more engaged' is not specific enough to be effective. Instead, your goal might be 'I want you to do X, Y, and Z' (where X, Y, and Z are measurable indicators of engagement, such as attending all meetings, following up all actions, etc.). Make sure your goal is achievable within the time bounds. If you've only got half an hour with someone, make sure your goal can be achieved by the time you part ways.

> A client of mine, Kate, was preparing for a meeting with her boss, and it was a big one. She wasn't happy with the way her boss was treating her, and wanted to use this meeting to let her know. As we prepared for the session I asked how long she would have. She said, '30 minutes... but my boss is always running late.' So we needed to tailor the messaging to achieve her objective within *less* than 30 minutes.

STEP 2: Understand the context.

> Kate had established a goal, but we quickly realised that the goal didn't quite fit in with the context that led to the meeting and what her boss was expecting – that is, a performance review discussion. Yes, Kate was frustrated, but the context wasn't right to deal with that right now. Realising that a good performance review and subsequent pay rise was the most critical and time-sensitive goal, we refined the goal and our influence strategy. We distinguished between the short-term, immediate need and the longer-term, higher need.

So ask yourself:

- What is my ultimate high-level goal (the long term goal as opposed to the goal of this meeting)?
- What is the context that surrounds that goal?

STEP 3: Understand the other person.

Understand the other person and how they are similar or different to you. Empathy is key here.

- What are the things that matter to them?
- What is in your control that you can offer or take away? Do they need time, support, credit, political cover, money, access, training, mentoring, control, autonomy, gifts? (I'm not talking about a bribe, but an offer of genuine assistance.)
- What do you share in common?
- What vision will get them excited?
- What is their preferred communication style?

What else do you know about this person that you can incorporate into the 'what', 'how', or 'why' you communicate with them? What matters to them? What do they value?

> As I worked with Kate, we realised that her boss was in an uncertain position of her own. Her boss wasn't an experienced people leader and so had her own insecurities around delegation and the perceived need to know everything. There was lots of change going on within their organisation, which only added to her boss' concerns. Kate's boss needed certainty and to look good amongst her colleagues. She was less interested in helping her team.
>
> Knowing this information in advance of the performance review conversation was extremely helpful for Kate. It helped Kate gain a better understanding of her boss, and we talked about how she could use this to influence the trajectory of the meeting. This was invaluable knowledge that Kate kept front of mind as she prepared for the meeting. Kate would not let her boss' needs undermine her own.

You see, it's what happens at the intersection between mindset and communication that determines our presence and defines our leadership brand. When we understand our own needs also our audience's needs, we can more effectively choose how we behave and what language we use. This informs people's perceptions of us and determines whether we have the executive presence that we seek.

So understanding your preferences, others' preferences and what that means for how you can communicate for influence is absolutely paramount for success.

STEP 4: Select an approach.

Approach is everything. 'It's not what you say, it's how you say it!' When determining our approach, we need to recognise the difference between appealing to the left (facts and data) or right brain (emotions and experiences) of our audience. Which one we should aim to appeal to comes down to the goal we want to achieve. To show you what I mean, let's consider four different approaches, based on four different goals.

- If you want to get *intellectual* understanding on an issue, you will focus on left-brain language, providing facts and data as support. We often default to this, mistakenly thinking it's all that matters. But if we are to use influential communication to get what we want, it needs to be about more than facts. We need to think about wants, needs, desires, dreams.

- If we need someone to *comply* with something, we need to assert ourselves and support our request by being clear about consequences, positive and negative. If you feel that asserting isn't the right approach and you need to negotiate, the key is to listen to their needs. Take the time to consider and understand a range of options and alternatives.

- If you really want someone to be *committed* to something, appeal to their heart. Be clear on what it means to them. Listen and be genuine. Be willing to be vulnerable and commit to a collaborative solution.

- If you want to get your team or your board *inspired*, you have to mix it up. Use a combination of right-brain language (emotion, possibility), spirit (shared experiences and beliefs), and vision (shared vision) to get them across the line.

> For Kate's meeting, we went with a primarily left-brain approach. We decided it was most important to be prepared with the facts around her performance and how that contributed to her boss achieving her objectives.

STEP 5: Get specific.

This is planning at its most detailed. It's pulling together your agenda and playing out all the different potential scenarios. In the example with Kate, we played out the scenario that her boss would arrive with only five minutes to spare.

Yes, I am suggesting that for each meeting you have, you have an agenda. Because, let's be honest, how many meetings have you attended that were just a waste of your time? It's disrespectful and inefficient to come to a meeting unprepared. If you have an agenda, even a rough one, for every one of your meetings, you will not only stop wasting time, you will earn more respect from your colleagues and seniors. An agenda is effectively a running order for your meeting, getting into the specifics of how it is likely to go.

Ask yourself:

- What is my opening?
- What questions will they ask and what objections will they raise?
- How will I address their objections?
- What is the real question or issue that needs to be addressed? How will I approach the elephants in the room?
- How will I know when I have achieved my goal?
- How will I avoid getting lost in rabbit warrens and unnecessary detail?
- What will I do to ensure current issues are not steamrolled by new ones?

Why go into this level of detail? You're making sure there's enough time to cover what you need to, taking into account the dialogue (yes, two-way conversation!) that needs to take place. You'd be surprised how many meetings fail to achieve their objectives simply because nobody has made the effort to put together a detailed plan. Don't fall into this trap!

STEP 6: Prepare.

Preparation is one of the most underrated, undervalued, and therefore underutilised enablers for women in finance. I've covered my proactive approach to time in a previous chapter, so I'll just get really practical here and share a few tips on how to prepare for high-stakes meetings.

First: Let yourself vent!

Vent for two minutes, uncensored. I love this one. Think about a difficult conversation you know you're going to have in the coming weeks. Now, in a private spot, imagine this person is in front of you, and say whatever it is you'd really like to say to them. #nofilter! Swear, tell them where to go, let them know what you really think of them. Just get it out!

This is such a powerful tool, and you can literally do this 'prep' in two minutes. In those two minutes, you rid yourself of all the pent-up emotion and negative energy that you know won't serve you in the meeting. Better to get it out in practice than in person! The other thing that makes this such a great tool is that you might actually come up with something sensible. You might end up thinking, 'Why don't I just say that to them?'

> Kate had lots of feedback she wanted to give her boss, yet she knew she was going to be the only one receiving feedback in this particular meeting. So for her, the step of venting was absolutely critical. She needed to get a lot off her chest so that she wouldn't be distracted from her more important purpose in the meeting.

Give it a go. It adds a huge amount of value in a short amount of time – and it's fun!

Second: Don't get too caught up in the detail.

Start big picture, and get detailed from there. My finance leaders often get caught up in the detail, and that confuses them and causes them stress. They're so worried about being faced with a question they don't know the answer to that they focus all their energy on the subtleties of the subject matter instead of looking at the overarching meaning behind it. The key here is to be really clear and articulate about the big-picture context and purpose, then cascade into the detail from there.

Now I want to give you a few specific tips around the best way to practise.

- Practise your crisp opening: your 'snappy start', as my daughters call it. You know what they say: If you don't get them in the first 10 seconds (and that's being generous), you've lost them. First impressions count.

- Practise objections. You probably know what they're going to be, so don't use them as excuses. Use them to help you prepare. Find ways to work around them. Think about how you can make the person comfortable with whatever you are proposing.

- Practise being adaptive with your approach. Whatever you think you know about their preferred style, they may still surprise you! Even if you don't get to apply it this time, practising different approaches improves your communication flexibility and quick thinking, so it's well worth the effort.

- For really big meetings, as cringeworthy as it may sound, I would recommend that you videotape or record your practice sessions and play them back. There are some things you just don't pick up on until you see them from a third-person perspective.

Rehearsing is so important. One of the greatest benefits of rehearsing is that it maximises the clarity of your requests. And if you're not clear on what you want, you can be sure no one else is! Be clear and don't let the effectiveness of your impact come down to chance.

STEP 7: Debrief, reflect, and revise.

I'm sure you've been involved in enough projects to know that debrief meetings are good governance. However, if they aren't executed and facilitated well, they can feel like no more than a tick-the-box exercise – or even a flat-out waste of time. However, a considered debrief and appropriate reflection and implementation of new actions is worth its weight in gold. It doesn't need to be long – it just needs to achieve the objective of helping team members to learn and grow from the experience.

We don't tend to think about our performance in meetings, or our expectations of that performance. So let me be clear: You should. Just as a sports team expects to be better with every game they play, you should expect to be more effective with every meeting you attend. Consider how many meetings you have in a week. Now think about the increase in performance and increase in impact you could have if you took a more purposeful approach to those meetings. The debrief allows for you to execute on that intent.

Simply ask yourself:

- What worked and what didn't?
- What was the gap and how can I close it?
- What are the next steps, and how do I implement that learning going forward?

Another common approach is stop/start/continue. What should you *stop* doing, what should you *start* doing, and what should you *continue* doing? Whichever approach works best for you, just go with that. Because even if you implement all the preparation I've described in steps 1–6, you will never be able to entirely predict how another person will behave, and there are no guarantees as to the outcome of any conversation. Sometimes it will go your way and sometimes it won't, and the debrief is how we learn and grow from that.

> Kate received a glowing performance review. She walked out with great feedback, a bonus, and a pay rise. She was really happy with how the meeting went, and she had achieved her objective. Because we had already planned for future conversations with her boss (the upward feedback she wanted to give), she was able to execute on this one perfectly without sacrificing herself or her integrity to do so.

Communicating for impact is about more than just the words

Communication is the culmination of our mindset, attitudes, and behaviours. It's the tip of the iceberg that sits above the water line. It's how we articulate our vision and goals, it's how we engage with the people around us, and it's how we achieve success. Counterintuitively, good communication is often about thinking more and talking less. It's about listening more, and assuming less.

When we take a proactive approach to our communication, we have far more impact than when we 'wing it'. When we have impact, we have executive presence. When we have executive presence, people approach us with new opportunities. We are held up as role models for other women in finance and become an integral part of retaining and attracting women in the business.

When you approach each meeting using the 7-step approach, your productivity within these meetings will increase, and you will establish a new quality benchmark for your team's meetings. By upping the standards of communication in an area that is typically renowned for weak communication, your impact on performance effectiveness can be exponential.

9 BRING CHANGE TO LIFE

> "Courage is contagious. Every time we choose courage, we make everyone around us a little better and the world a little braver."
>
> *Brené Brown*

In recent years, many organisations have introduced 'women in leadership' programs. Diversity and inclusion groups are being built to champion this change. We're starting to see some really impactful International Women's Day events. Obviously, I think that's all absolutely awesome. What worries me, however, is how effective those programs and initiatives are. Time and time again, I hear a familiar narrative: 'What we're doing isn't working. We still can't attract women to our organisation. The senior female leaders that went through the leadership program have left. Our diversity group has disintegrated.'

What we're doing isn't working.

We need to do more

I understand, it isn't an easy change. But I heard recently that someone — a lady, no less – said in a leadership meeting, 'This lady isn't performing, and it's probably no surprise because we know that being part-time doesn't work in this job.' Even after all the trails that women before us have blazed, women are still denying other women the simple freedom to balance work with life. Clearly, we still have a long way to go.

If we are to attract, develop, and retain women in finance, we need to do more, because the existing women in leadership initiatives in finance aren't working.

These women in leadership programs in and of themselves are generally very good – the women involved ('the cohort') learn useful skills and develop good relationships. The change is, however, that the work the cohort undertakes happens in isolation.

So, practically speaking, the woman in finance is thinking: 'Great, I've been accepted into this women-in-leadership program. I'm going to have to make up those two hours a week elsewhere. I have meetings on either side of the workshop… phew, I'll be running to *and* from it.' From there, the thought process can easily spiral to: 'I'd better not flag to my boss that I'm taking two hours out of my day to attend this; he might ask me not to go,' or 'I have no time to implement any of this great stuff I'm learning,' or 'This work is useless anyway, because my boss doesn't care.'

As I've shared earlier in this book, once you start to believe something, your brain will search for data in your environment to support it. That's why it saddens me to see women go through a coaching program or leadership training program only to resign shortly thereafter. I mean, it's great that these women have newfound confidence and clarity around their values, what they're going to do, and how they're going to do it. They leave feeling incredibly empowered, and it's all thanks to the great work they've done with their coach or trainer (and to the sponsor who put them on the program to begin with).

But when these great women walk out the door, so does their contribution to the fabric of the corporate culture. And we desperately need their contribution. The female talent that walks out the door is often the talent companies most need to keep, because they represent the best of the company. They are the ones that truly live the values of the organisation: not only of equality, diversity, and inclusion, but also of innovation, challenging the status quo and raising the bar.

So what's missing?

One of the key missing elements in our organisational culture is exactly what we've been talking about through these past few chapters: what I call 'conversations to create change'. These are the conversations where the leader is learning about herself, her strengths, her needs, and what she should expect from a good leader and good team. They're the conversations where she realises there is room for improvement in the department, in her boss, in her team, and in herself. And they're even the conversations after that, where she suspects that what she's been saying hasn't been heard and she needs to say it again.

This is what's missing. The ability to have real conversations to create change.

What is a conversation to create change?

It is the culmination of everything in this book. It is a conversation you have to create the change you want. It is a conversation you are finally equipped to have now that you have found your purpose, identified the change you want to see, and thought strategically about how you want to execute on that purpose in your current role and organisation. It is a conversation that will give your work real meaning and allow you to share it proudly.

A conversation to create change is a specific type of influence conversation, and it can follow the same structure from the previous chapter. The key element is that the goal is to influence a change that will move you toward your vision.

Once you have identified what revs you up, you can have a conversation that will help you structure your work to align with your motivators and not against them. Despite all the change and uncertainty in your context, you *are* ready to have this conversation.

This is the first in a series of conversations to create change – conversations that will move you forward, step by step, toward your vision.

If you want to see change, you must take responsibility for having these conversations. And you can feel comfortable doing this, because you have a strong powerbase around you. You can be confident in the way you communicate, because you are clear about how your work creates value and you can clearly distinguish it from work that doesn't have impact.

These are the conversations that will help you make real changes toward your vision, changes that can make a meaningful impact exactly where you're at. These conversations have a high chance of success, because you are having them in a way that is collaborative, helpful, and respectful – not delivering ultimatums. These conversations are your path to deepening your relationships with others, helping them understand how you can help each other, and showing them the role they have to play in opening doors for women in finance. This is how you can *successfully influence one person at a time*.

How do I know what change I want?

I was previously mentored by Jen Rufati, Chief Executive Women Scholarship winner. She drew up the following diagram to demonstrate how she viewed her career trajectory. She said that if we know where we are now, and we know where we want to be, then our job is simply to make sure that the decisions we make about our work and our career move us forward toward our vision, one step at a time.

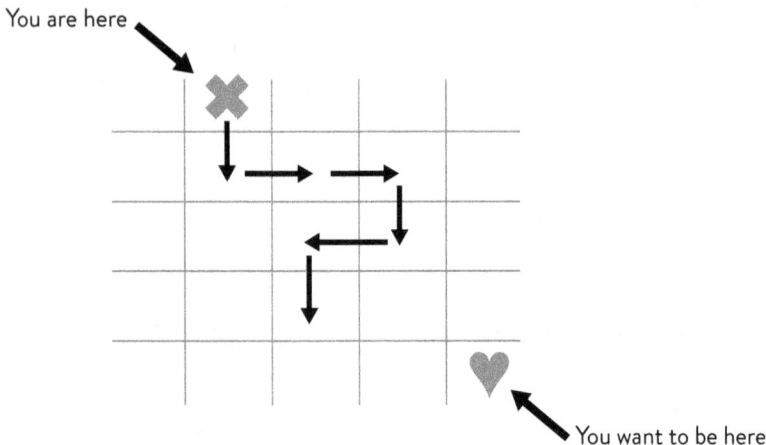

What I love about this approach is that it reflects the non-linearity of the modern career trajectory. In our increasingly matrixed organisations, new roles are being created almost every month. In this rapidly changing context, none of us can know with 100% certainty what our ultimate path, or even our next move, will be. It's a common mistake to think that we need to know exactly what our future holds, and that if we don't, we've failed. Know where you want to end up, but stay flexible about how you're going to get there.

Sometimes it is the role you didn't think you wanted, or get asked to do that provides you with a set of skills that ultimately sets you up for that future success. For Jen it was understanding what excited her in a role and what did she love to do – because then it didn't really feel like work.

In this book, I've tried to solve for you the biggest problem many women in finance face, and that's not knowing your end game. After all the work you've done, you still may not have a specific role in mind, but you should have a clear sense of purpose and the characteristics you will have as you carry out that purpose. And you have the mindset, behaviours, and capabilities you need to confidently move across the grid and down to that bottom-right corner.

Conversations are more than just talk

In order for conversations to create change, they need to cover the right material in the right way. What you need to cover will vary depending on where you stand relative to your vision, and where your organisation is at in relation to gender diversity. Throughout this book I have given you statistics, common scenarios, case studies and other evidence that you can use in your conversations to create change.

Broadly speaking, you need to cover:

- *Why?* Why is gender diversity and inclusion important to your organisation? Having an inherent sense that 'It's the right thing to do' is great, but you need to be able to verbalise the importance of inclusion. Use the strategic thinking skills you learned in earlier chapters.

- *What?* What does gender equality look like for your organisation? Think about their policies and targets. What strategies or practices can be implemented to set women up for success?

- *Where?* Where does your organisation want to position itself with regard to gender issues? Where in the organisation does responsibility for diversity or authority to act really lie?

- *When?* Is gender diversity a high priority relative to other strategic initiatives, and how does this influence the timing of implementation?

- *How?* What is the best way to tackle the change you want to initiate and deliver incremental and sustained success? How does it fit in the organisational context (answered in the four previous questions)? And most importantly, how can you help the organisation through this very important change?

If you are embarking on a conversation to initiate change (on gender or otherwise), here are the key elements you need to tick off to be sure that these conversations are worth having:

- ❏ You have clearly defined the change you want to see.
- ❏ You understand how the change will move you toward your vision.
- ❏ The change is time bound, so that it cannot simply be put off.
- ❏ The change has identifiable, tangible characteristics, so you will know when it has occurred.
- ❏ The change will positively contribute to your performance in your current job.

These five elements are critical, because none of us has the time, energy, or patience to keep on beating a dead horse. We need to engage the reward system in our brain – to allow quick wins to create momentum. Because when we create momentum through continued wins, we feel like we're building something. And the natural consequence of that is confidence – something most women desperately want to build or regain when they feel like they've lost their way in this male-dominated industry.

Possibly for the first time, you now understand *what* you're doing and *why* you're doing it. Better still, you've know *how* to do it in order to get the results you want. You finally feel like you fit in without wearing a mask – and it feels good! But it's not enough. We need to continue to chip away at the dominant masculine culture. We need to initiate and contribute to conversations that will create the change not just for us, but for all the women who come after us.

The role of courage

I understand that we want to believe that we will be measured, assessed and promoted based on our results. So it would be tempting to take all the great learnings you have applied from reading this book and carrying out the activities I've included for you, and be comfortable that your results will speak for themselves. I hope you have also realised by now that that's not going to work. In order for you to create the change you want to see, in order for you to thrive, you need to step out of your comfort zone and be courageous. Having conversations to create change is a big part of that.

Professor James R. Detert, of University of Virginia's Darden School of Business uses the term 'competently courageous' to describe people who successfully speak up at work without negative consequences to their careers. Through his extensive research on workplace courage, he identifies 4 key principles that competently courageous[19] people apply consistently to create positive change in their workplace. These are:

> **Laying the groundwork:** Changemakers need to have established a good foundation of credibility and results (think of it as 'goodwill' on their employee balance sheet!) within their workplace before they challenge the system. Psychologists refer to this accumulated goodwill as idiosynchrasy credits, but you probably refer to this at work as a 'proven track record'. I think the challenge women in finance need to address in this area is not about whether you've done the groundwork; it's about who knows you've done the groundwork. Tall poppy syndrome in the workplace does not help. This is where your profile is important: peoples' perceptions about you, your leadership style and your achievements.
>
> **Choosing your battles:** We all know the saying, 'pick your battles' and the same applies when pushing for change. In Daniel Pink's most recent book, *When: The Scientific Secrets of Perfect Timing*[20] he challenges the notion that we need to "Start With Why" and says that we need to focus on "When". Throughout the book, he shares with us the research he has performed on timing throughout the day and the relationship with financial markets, he informs us to the best time of the day to work and how to take a 'nappuccino'. The fundamental premise, though, and the most important takeaway, is the

notion that we can do everything, just not at the same time. Be a master at good timing.

Persuading in the moment: Detert's 3 keys to effective persuasion are framing (context), using data effectively (content) and managing the emotion in the room (empathy). If you have read the previous chapters, you know how to do these things. If you have done the meta activity: Integrate Your Purpose, you also know how to integrate those activities *now* so you can use them in an instant.

Following up: Competently courageous people are good finishers. They follow up well beyond their moment of action and this is what improves their credibility and respect across the business *even* if they haven't succeeded in the change this time around. Their goodwill balance goes up. I think women have the advantage here. Typically higher on humility as an inherent characteristic, women can more naturally leverage this. Whilst there may be a fear of admitting you've failed, as research professor and bestselling author Brené Brown explains in her work, embracing vulnerability is the key to growth, deeper relationships and new levels of performance. Competently courageous women can play a huge role in introducing a culture of vulnerability into their team.

Creating change is hard. But I also know when you're anchored to purpose and you have the capability, you can be confident in your approach and stand in conviction even when it's hard.

Who do you need to have these conversations with?

You are a seriously powerful woman right now! You have so much in your leadership toolbelt. I truly hope you feel this. There are a myriad of conversations that you are now equipped to have in order to create change. Here are just a few:

- With your boss
- With your team
- With your organisation's women-in-leadership advisory board
- With the men and women you work with
- With junior women in finance
- With junior men in finance
- With your clients
- With the business
- With conference delegates (yes, I am challenging you to speak at conferences!)

What role can your powerbase play in these conversations.? Are they conduits for these conversations? Do you need to arm them with information to help them have conversations to create change? Do this, and you can influence the influencers!

If we engage as many components of the system in this conversation as
possible, and actively create change wherever we can, we can accelerate and amplify our impact.

Imagine a still, calm pond with no ripples or current. Now you start throwing pebbles into it, one at a time. They are small, and it is just you throwing them. And yet, the ripples travel far and wide. What I love about this analogy is that although the ripples seem to spread out from the drop point, what's really happening is that the individual water molecules displaced by the pebble are just moving back and forth in place. Every action you take, no matter how small, creates a ripple effect. Know that you are a part of something bigger, and use that to create change.

9.1 META ACTIVITY 3: CREATE MASTERY THROUGH PURPOSE

We have talked about so many concepts throughout this book! I have done my best to share as much as I can in just one book, using the results from my women in finance clients to determine what will be most impactful for you and what can wait. I wanted to provide you with every opportunity to gain clarity, generate insight, observe different perspectives and catapult into action. You are now equipped with new skills, tools and techniques that enable you to focus on what matters as you achieve your career goals.

Now I'd like to help you bring it all together in a way that allows it to 'land' in your brain in a coherent way. In a way that will guarantee you amplify your impact at work and execute your purpose exactly where you're at. As I've said to you before, you need to know where you're going if you want to effectively implement what you have learned. I'll do that right now with the Impact Effect.

The Impact Effect

The Impact Effect simply describes for you the transformations that you will undergo when you do this work. When you consider the shifts that you can make, as listed in the table below, it is no wonder that your performance will be elevated to mastery level! In doing so, your leadership identify will really be elevated and you will be perceived exactly as you want. Cross check these descriptors to those that you identified in 'Your leadership style' from Meta activity 1: Connect to your purpose.

	FROM	TO	BOOK CHAPTER
ENERGY	Friction	'Fifth gear'	*Light up your motivators*
MINDSET	Cautious	Confident	*Remove your mask*
LEVEL OF SATISFACTION	Frustrated	Fulfilled	*Plan for purpose*
STATE	Reactive	Proactive	*Own your impact*
RELATIONSHIPS	Transactional	Impactful	*Establish your powerbase*
FOCUS OF ATTENTION	Siloed	Strategic	*Do what matters*
PRESENTATIONS	Isolated	Empowered	*Present with confidence*
COMMUNICATION	Inform	Influence	*Communicate for influence*
CHANGE	'done to me'	'created for me'	*Bring change to life*

Use the Impact Effect to know which chapters of this book you need to revisit as you navigate through the challenges and opportunities you are faced with at work.

The Identity Iceberg

Throughout this book I have given you the building blocks to helping you achieve results beyond the numbers. What those results are depends on you and your purpose. The chapters have been specifically ordered in such a way that the knowledge gained and actions applied build on each other in a coherent way. At the highest level, this is what it looks like:

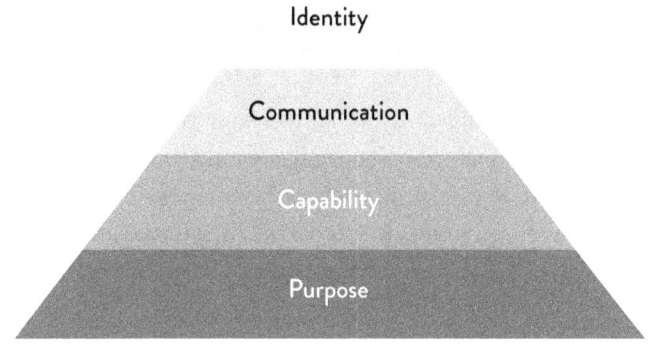

Your purpose underpins everything you do and makes meaning of every activity you undertake. This is at the core of Section 1, *Aspiration*. It fuels your engine, sets your direction and drives you forward to achieve your vision and mission. You will recall that in Meta activity 1: *Connect to your purpose* you identified skills, relationships and ways of working that would help you achieve your vision.

These form the basis of Section 2, *Attributes*, of the book. In this section, we covered the key capabilities that women in finance need to draw upon in mind, attitude and behaviour in order to do the work in a way that will allow you to perform with purpose and progress your career toward your vision. In Meta activity 2: *Integrate your purpose*, I shared with you the key model that will enable you to integrate everything you do into your work exactly where you're at.

Section 3, *Approach,* took it to the next level as we got really practical in how we would deliver results through our purpose. We focused on communication as the mode that allows our defined purpose and developed capabilities to become 'visible'. Communication is the first level that sits above the water line, if we continue the commonly used iceberg analogy. It is the vehicle through which we create the changes we need, in order to achieve our vision. We need to know how to present, how to influence and how to create change through conversation.

This leaves us with the tip of the iceberg. How do we pull together and package up all you've learned and discovered about yourself through this book? It's you. You and your identity.

In Meta activity 1: *Connect to your purpose*, you identified attributes and behaviours as observed by others that would be indicative of your leadership style were you to achieve your vision. This activity is intended to allow you to revisit that part of the exercise and further refine it based on the remainder of the book.

Your Impactful Identity

If you want to amplify your impact you need to ensure that your leadership characteristics have the impact you want them to have. Whether it be to deliver a message, move you forward or stop a limiting behaviour, the characteristics that form the basis of your identity need to have impact.

You need to know the following:

Desired leadership characteristics: These are the qualities or features that form the basis of your leadership identity. They may come in the form of a mindset or attitude that you adopt, a value or preference that is important to you, or a behaviour or competency that you demonstrate. When you are doing this self-reflection work, keep your desired leadership characteristics manageable. Focus on the ones that will set you apart from others and help you move towards your purpose most effectively. You know what they say, you don't want to be the jack of all trades and the master of none! Identify the characteristics that will have the greatest impact and shift the dial for you.

How the characteristic links to your purpose: Once you have identified your purpose it's like a weight has been lifted off your shoulders and there is a lightness about your energy. If we are going to intentionally create our identity, we want to make sure we are only introducing characteristics that are congruent with achieving our purpose.

How the characteristic will improve your performance: We want to create an identity that works for us exactly where we are at: that is, in our current job. So we also need to make sure that there is a direct correlation between our existing responsibilities so we can be confident that it will improve our performance and help us progress.

How to measure our impact: Development of characteristics can be hard to measure if we don't intentionally do so. Knowing how

DESIRED LEADERSHIP CHARACTERISTIC	LINK TO PURPOSE	LINK TO PERFORMANCE	METRIC TO MEASURE	ACTION(S) REQUIRED	POWERBASE ASSISTANCE REQUIRED
(List the elements of your leadership identity you want to embody. Think about how you want people to perceive you and what other qualities or features you want to stand out.)	(How will this characteristic help you achieve your vision/ deliver your purpose?)	(How will this characteristic help you perform better in your current job?)	(How will you know you have implemented and embedded this leadership characteristic into your identity?)	(What action do you need to take to implement this characteristic? Do you need to learn something, strengthen something, let go of something?)	(Who's experience or help can you draw on to help you take action immediately and more effectively?)

your desired leadership characteristics link to your purpose and performance, it's now time to identify how you will know that you have implemented and embedded this characteristic effectively. Use a criteria that is easy to measure either quantitatively (e.g. "I get results first time with little rework") or qualitatively (e.g. "My client approaches me proactively for help").

What action you need to take: Quite simply, this is what you need to do to make it happen. Be as specific as possible, and feel free to incorporate it into a series of steps that you can check off one by one.

Powerbase assistance required: I guarantee that the action you need to take has been taken or can be learned from someone. If you want to incorporate a particular leadership characteristic with a level of urgency, I strongly recommend that you proactively seek assistance from your powerbase. This will get you there faster and with the benefit of their own experience and expertise.

What to do now

Draw the table on page 113 in a notepad or download it from my website: www.alenabennett.com.au

Reflection questions

Imagine you are re-reading this book in 12 months from now. In that time, you have successfully embedded the above desired leadership characteristics into your impactful identity. Consider the following:

- ❏ What have you achieved? What steps have you taken towards your vision and living through your purpose?
- ❏ How does it feel?
- ❏ How has this achievement influenced other aspects of your work and life?

❏ How would you describe yourself now?

❏ How do others describe you now?

❏ What does your future now look like?

Knowing what you're about to embark on, knowing the changes you want to create for yourself, and knowing the keys to success, I want to share with you one final tool. It's called the *Impact System*.

Introducing the Impact System

The Impact System combines all the elements that you need to create the change you want to see. Simply put, the Impact System is what sits between a request (an 'ask') and you getting the outcome (the 'approval'). It is the enabler to amplifying your impact.

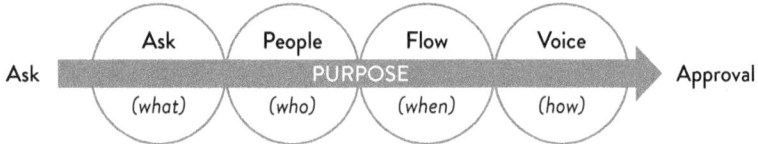

The five components of the Impact System

To get from ask to approval, you must acknowledge the correlation between all the elements. If you neglect to include a component of the Impact System, approval of your ask becomes very unlikely. Let's take a look at each component in turn.

The ask

Your 'ask' is basically what you want. Whether it be to learn a new capability or skill, to develop a new relationship or to get to a specific outcome, your ask needs to be clear so that everyone involved knows exactly what you want and what they need to do to get you there. That clarity includes not just *what* you're asking for but also *when* you need it and *why* you are asking for it. If you want to speed things up and get to approval quickly, you may also include suggestions on *how* they might deliver on your ask. Surprisingly, we are not very good at asking for things, especially when we think we won't get them. We hide behind our hesitancy, and this helps no one. Get your ask right.

The people

Moving through the Impact System quickly is largely dependent on getting *individuals* over the line quickly. If you are the one with the ask, it's your responsibility to identify all the different people that will need to be included in the chain. Do this first, as part of your Impact System planning, because the type and timing of any conversation should always be based on the person you are conversing with. You also want to give yourself as much time as possible to establish new relationships before you need them so that they can work most effectively for you.

The flow

In order to make the Impact System flow, you need to consider context and timing. Have you ever swum in a highly chlorinated pool wearing sterling silver? It turns dull and grey. You don't want the same thing happening to your influence conversations because something in the environment is tarnishing your efforts. Nor, of course, do you want to miss the boat entirely. There's nothing worse than having everything teed up and ready to go, only to find out that the CEO is away for a month! Be proactive about taking timing and context into account, and incorporate this into your Impact System.

The voice

This is the key factor in moving through the Impact System successfully. We need to make each conversation count. And here's the thing. You can nail *your* conversations, but the minute you leave a critical conversation to someone else, you run the risk of it falling flat and quashing the entire process.

Imagine one of your direct reports comes to you with a great initiative. You're sold – this is definitely something worth exploring. So you take it to one of your peers and say, 'Hey, what do you think?' They agree that it's got legs, and you ask them to progress it because it largely sits in their space. But as good an idea as it is, the initiative dies. Why? Simple. Your peer wasn't able to have a good influence conversation with the next person in the approval process.

You need to take the proactive action to control the voice at every step, or you risk the system breaking down.

Your purpose

Your purpose runs through the core of the Impact System: it is the spine. You need to be able to make meaning of each and every change in the context of your purpose. Connecting to purpose is the very thing what will create results for you that are transformational rather than transactional. This can be hard, which is why I have shared with you throughout this book how to break down your purpose into meaningful and actionable chunks.

When you can't get follow-through after initial buy-in to a project

Have you ever had the experience where someone *seems* to buy in to your project wholeheartedly, but never follows through? Where do you think the Impact System broke down? Most people blame the person that didn't follow through, saying something like, 'They didn't prioritise my project.' That, dear reader, is an excuse. Prioritisation means determining what's most important, and that dictates timing. The person didn't follow through on your project because, based on the information they had, they just didn't think it was important enough. And that's on you.

Maybe it's just not the right time for the initiative you've asked for – you got the *flow* wrong. But – and this is where things get a bit challenging and controversial – quite often, our timing *is* right. It was something else that was wrong. And it's up to you to do the work to correct that.

Where we often go wrong

There are a whole lot of common mistakes we make at each component of the Impact System. Have a look at the following list, and check off the ones you think might be holding you back. Remember, this is not a tool to beat yourself up with! It's a tool to work out how you can unblock the pathway from 'ask' to 'approve':

The ask
- ❏ Not being clear on the why
- ❏ Not appealing strongly enough to the other party's why, or the organisation's why
- ❏ Not being clear about the benefits of what you're asking for

The people
- ❏ Asking the wrong people
- ❏ Making an incorrect assumption around someone's decision making authority

The flow
- ❏ Getting the timing wrong
- ❏ Forgetting or not recognising another business issue lurking in the background

The voice
- ❏ Not preparing well for your conversation
- ❏ Not executing the conversation well

- ❏ Not preparing other parties for the conversation
- ❏ Not setting aside enough time

Your purpose
- ❏ Not reconciling the ask to your purpose
- ❏ Not approaching change with the right attitude and mindset
- ❏ Not breaking down your purpose into realistic steps to incorporate into the ask

What we need to do instead

We need to combine strategic, tactical and practical thinking when it comes to tackling the Impact System. If we want to move from ask to approval quickly and maximise our chance of success, we need to take a systems thinking approach.

Below is a short guide to help you plan for your next initiative. Brainstorm the key components of your Impact System and use this to drive the actions you need to create the change that will work for you.

A soft copy of this template can be found on my website at www.alenabennett.com.au.

The ask
- ❏ What is the initiative? What change do you want?
- ❏ What outcome are you looking for and how does this align with your purpose?*
- ❏ What does is look like?
- ❏ When do you want it?
- ❏ How does it fit in with the organizational vision/mission/strategy (the *why*)?

- ❏ How does it fit in with the individual *why*s of the people in the system?

The people
- ❏ Who are the individuals involved in the approval process and the individuals that support them?
- ❏ How far alone on the change journey ('the journey') are they, or do you need to take them 'on the journey'?
- ❏ Who are the people that usually hold things up?
- ❏ Who are the people that usually distract others' from moving forward?
- ❏ Who are the key individuals that can fast track approval?

The flow
- ❏ What is the current context of the organisation and impacted departments?
- ❏ Is there a difference between the current context and the expected future contexts?
- ❏ What are the relevant time points and milestones? (Use the information from 'The people' as a guide.)
- ❏ What other things are going on that may impact timing for the individuals involved?
- ❏ Are we confident in our timing?*

The voice
- ❏ Have you prepared a clear agenda for the conversations or presentations involved that maximises your chance of success?
- ❏ Have you prepared for your conversations with the right mindset, attitudes and perspectives that will help you deliver your message?*

- ❏ Is there a clear purpose for each conversation that needs to occur throughout the system?

- ❏ Does everyone involved in the system have the communication skills required to successfully execute their part?

*considerations related to 'Your Purpose'. These must be integrated *into* the system and not stand alone.

And remember, use your powerbase as you prepare for this work! Getting them involved sharing their ideas and perspectives will increase your chance of success.

Amplifying your impact by creating change that is realistic, easy and impactful may sound easy to do, but in practice it can be seriously challenging to implement. Understanding and using both the Impact Effect and the Impact System will ensure that when you start something, you can feel confident in getting the support and action you need to get it finished. Most importantly, that all of this work is in congruence with your Impactful Identity!

FINAL WORDS

I wrote this book for you because I believe that all women in finance have it within themselves to find their purpose, take action, and achieve their dreams. And, in so doing, to make a difference to women in finance everywhere. I've worked with, for, and alongside enough amazing women in finance to know that with a bit of investment in ourselves and our capabilities, *we* are the ones who will change the game.

As a group, we are drastically underappreciated, underutilised, and unused to asking for help. I can't tell you how many times I've heard, 'I've just lost a bit of confidence. I'd love to do something just for me. I don't want to still feel this way in 12 months.' But still we get up, go to work, buck up, put our heads down, and get the job done. And nothing ever really seems to change.

Until now.

With this book, I want to give you the tools and inspiration to find your purpose and achieve your vision. I want to help you create the space within your current role to develop the capabilities you need to achieve that vision. I want to give you the platform and voice to speak up and have the necessary conversations to create the change you want to see. I want to give you the confidence to step into new roles – roles that will help you make a bigger contribution to the world. Roles you might not even think you're capable of. I want to give you everything you need to change the world.

When you experience the ultimate satisfaction that comes with knowing and executing on your purpose, exactly where you're at, everything falls into place. How do I know? Because everything I share in this book I teach and implement myself.

Well done on getting this far. Also, saddle up! Because you now have a choice: What will you do with the information you now have? With that choice comes responsibility – the responsibility to join me and all the other change makers in amplifying the impact of women in finance so that we can finally achieve the equality that should have been there all along. My greatest hope is that this message spreads beyond us as individuals to contribute to the growth of women in finance everywhere.

That is what delivering results beyond the numbers is all about. It's taking amazing women with amazing skills and amazing aspirations and enabling them to use 100% of their capability. Elevating them beyond the back office, beyond the sea of blue chambray shirts! How do we can do this? By appreciating that meaning matters.

When Moana finally leaned into her purpose, she embarked on a journey that almost cost her life more than once. But her strength of conviction meant that she didn't consider an alternative. She learned how to become a wayfinder, how to stand up to those bigger and stronger than her. How to follow her dreams. And when she returned to become Queen, she lifted Motonui to a place of abundance unlike anything it had ever experienced.

Finding your purpose when you're surrounded by numbers, men, and deadlines *is* possible. It doesn't need to be this big, overwhelming process. And it doesn't mean you need to walk away from the amazing career you've worked so hard to develop. Far from it. You simply need to commit to do the practical work to identify your purpose – your vision. You need to find the common thread between that and where you are now. This is your lightbulb moment, where it all comes together and you realise that you are on track, after all. From here, identifying the steps that will move you closer to your end game and finding the people you need to support you in those next steps becomes that much easier.

Find your purpose, and integrate it into what you are currently doing and where you're currently at. Because no one has the time, space, or energy to start all over again.

When we all do this work, have these insights, take these steps, and make these connections, together we are stronger. We can shift the paradigm, so we are no longer talking about the number of seats women occupy around the exec table, the number of female applicants to a job, or the mass exodus at the mid-senior level of leadership where women realise 'this place is just not for me.' And we're certainly not celebrating the fact that the proportion of female CFOs in Australia has increased from 12% to 16%! I mean, really! Progress is encouraging. But of itself, it's not enough. We are smart, savvy women, and we *can* change the face of finance. My role is to help you move from conversation to action. I've given you the very best of my programs, developed over many years of trial, error, and experience. I know you've got what you need to take the next step.

This is about more than us. It's about the fresh, eager women in this year's graduating class. It's about the young ladies studying economics and commerce at university. It's about our daughters in high school, trying to figure out what they want to do. It's about our daughters in primary school, who may one day want to be just like Mum. And it's also about our sons, brothers, and husbands. It's about helping them understand why we must amplify the impact of women in finance, and how they can help. It's about showing them how to have conversations that actively – no, better than that, *pro*actively – support us.

We *need* more women in finance. When we have greater representation of women in finance leadership roles, we have access to more of the best minds[21], which is at the very core of diversity and inclusion. When we can help women in finance find their voices and amplify their impact, we can speak as equals, improve outcomes, and do so in a more satisfying and fulfilled way.

We have the ability to help so many. Whether it's helping the business with the insights they need to achieve next quarter's performance targets, helping our clients make the best investment decisions or get through their next audit, or helping develop the financial literacy of females around the world, what we do is meaningful.

From local to global

In 2015, global leaders committed to 17 goals to achieve by 2030[22]. These goals were intended to end poverty, fight inequality and stop climate change. By reading this book and through the work you're doing, you are directly contributing to the achievement of UN Global Goal #5, Gender Equality. Specifically, you are working to achieve target 5.5: "Ensure full participation in leadership and decision making: Ensure women's full and effective participation and equal opportunities for leadership at all levels of decision-making in political, economic and public life." The work you are doing has meaning.

Meaning matters, and it always will, because it's the only thing that delivers long-term results.

I've covered a lot in this book! Here's a quick summary so that you can tick off the areas you feel confident in, and jump back into those you want another look at:

Part 1: Aspiration

- ❏ LEARN what motivates you at a subconscious level so you can implement practical changes to make the ship sail faster.
- ❏ REMOVE your mask by shifting your mindset and behaviours from change cautious to change confident.
- ❏ RECOGNISE why your purpose is so important as the driving force behind everything you do.

- ❏ DISCOVER your purpose and identify the key elements you need to work on to bring it to life.

Part 2: Attributes

- ❏ OWN your impact and take a proactive approach for success.
- ❏ ESTABLISH your powerbase so you have people around you to help get you where you want to go.
- ❏ CHOOSE to focus on the stuff that matters so you're not distracted by things that don't move you towards your purpose.
- ❏ CREATE opportunities to implement and practise your new mindset and behavioural capabilities in your current job.

Part 3: Approach

- ❏ LOVE presenting in front of people, knowing you can create great outcomes for you, your team, and your organisation.
- ❏ CONNECT people with purposeful change through powerful influence conversations.
- ❏ STEP UP and create the change you need to execute your purpose exactly where you're at.
- ❏ MASTER your impact by understanding how it all comes together in the impact system.

Do this work, and your performance will soar. You will deliver results you can't even begin to imagine right now, and I guarantee that they will extend way beyond the numbers. When you identify the meaning behind what you do, you can start to align your actions with that, and this allows you to make sense of the world in a very different way. Decisions become easier, pressures become lighter, and opportunities become greater. You operate in flow.

But you don't need to do it all today! Break it down as I've suggested, and take time to work on the capabilities and relationships that will support you. Don't be shy about sharing your newfound *why* with people – they will be inspired and will want to help you. Engage people in the right conversations, and you will create the change you want to see for yourself, your daughters, your sisters, and all the other awesome women in your present and future.

You are a change maker. Your meaning matters.

A NOTE TO ORGANISATIONS

This book is essentially a guidebook for women in finance who:

- want to work with purpose, but haven't yet articulated their purpose or vision
- want to build the critical capabilities to take the next step in their career
- want to regain confidence in what they're doing, how they're doing it, and how they present themselves within their organisation.

My career has focused on helping women identify their cause, improve their capabilities, and build their confidence so that they can work with purpose exactly where they are at. At the moment, we are seeing too many women assuming that the only way to reach their career goals is to quit the job that isn't currently helping them get there. This shouldn't be the norm.

The current trend of women in finance leaving their roles is causing pain for organisations because:

- There is attrition of women at all levels within an organisation, which puts undue pressure on remaining staff.
- Dramatically fewer women are rising up through the organisation, which reduces the number of female role models within the organisation.
- Women are less resilient to challenges because they don't feel the organisation is structured in a way to support them, and so retention becomes a challenge.

- The male-dominated culture and organisational identity is reinforced, which in turn influences recruitment.
- Attracting women into finance becomes challenging, introducing further stress to the gender-balance equation.
- Case studies and statistics indicate that initiatives to improve gender diversity in the workplace continue to be ineffective.

This is not just an issue for women

A male client of mine, John, took parental leave for both of his children in order to share the parental load with his wife (who is also a woman in finance). As a senior leader in an audit firm, he also experienced many of the same issues brought about by the unconscious bias and stigma that women in finance experience. He shared a specific conversation he had when he was talking to people about taking the time off – he was asked, "I thought you took your career seriously." I couldn't believe it. If this is the attitude that women in finance are up against then it is no wonder that they feel they need to walk on eggshells and not stand out. Through the lens of someone that had to reintegrate himself into work after his time off, he clearly saw how easy it was for women in finance to be 'excluded by design'. What he was referring to was not only the design of the firm policies themselves, but of the lazy, apathetic or simply uninformed way in which they were enforced. Now having returned from paternity leave, he realises he has to 'walk the talk' of the policies. He has to lead first and create a safer environment for women in finance to thrive. He is doing this through creating new roles that *can* be part time, that *can* be performed remotely and *can* flex up and down when busy season hits. His intent is that he can create his own ripple effect within the firm by proving within his sphere of control that change is possible.

The onus to create change doesn't rest solely with women. I believe that women are the ones who are in the best position to accelerate the process of turning companies into communities. However, they can't do it alone. We must engage all elements of the organisational ecosystem.

Influence happens one person at a time

Consider the following assumptions:

1. Every company has a diversity and inclusion policy pertaining to gender.
2. Company hierarchy is a pyramid, with the executive level of leadership at the point. Below that is a larger leadership team, who are then supported by a larger leadership team again, right down to the broad base of support staff.
3. Everyone has a line manager.

We'll assume all these assumptions are true, as this is reasonable for most organisations. It's all very well having policies, procedures, and structures in place to support women, but if each individual doesn't live by those policies, if they don't understand how they can practically implement and support them, then it's all for nought. That's why I believe the most important principle in empowering women in finance and promoting the conversations needed to create change is this:

Influence happens one person at a time and it needs to happen concurrently at all levels across an organisation.

In Chapter 9: Bring change to life, I talked about the cohorts of women that participate in leadership programs in their organisation. Specifically, I discussed how their work happens in isolation due in part to the absence of their ability to have 'conversations to create change'. However, there is a bigger picture that I want to touch on here. That is, the interaction between the cohort, the influencers, and the system.

This is a very simple illustration of how we need to integrate women in finance leadership programs into organisations if we want to create and sustain change. This book has been focused on giving a message to the women in finance – the cohort. But as you'll see, there are two other key factors in achieving fantastic outcomes around diversity and inclusion for an organisation. It's about also engaging the influencers and the system.

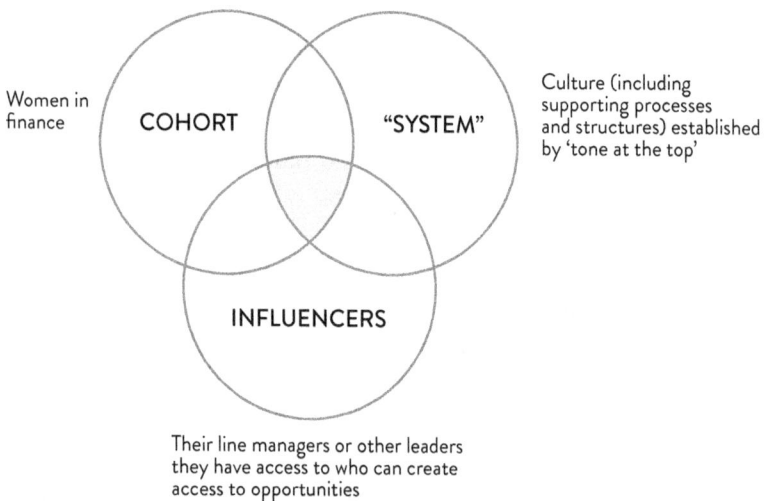

We need to connect all elements of the organisation. Empowering and mobilising the women in finance alone is not enough.

The role of influencers

In my opinion, 'influencers' are the most pivotal group in creating organisational change. These are the line managers or senior peers of women in finance, the group with the greatest strength in both seniority and numbers. These are the people who are in the best position to influence visible and measurable change. But they can't do it without the right skills.

Our influencers need to be able to have conversations that create change – both with female leaders and with execs. They need to be active translators, turning company policy into an active culture within their teams. They need to offer women in finance support and flexibility. They need to ask the right questions: 'What can I do to support you? How can I help you succeed? What opportunities can I open up for you?' They need to offer women a forum to ask questions without fear of judgment, ridicule, or consequence. They need to actively model best diversity and inclusion practices within the organisation, constantly asking themselves, 'What can I do to bring this to life?'

This is a lot to ask of a group that likely went through the ranks of the organisation when diversity and inclusion were vague, esoteric concepts. We are asking them to take a leading role in enabling change for women in finance when they are likely still learning themselves. So again, we need to empower them with the right skills and conditions to support women through conversation. In a sense, influencers are facing many of the same challenges women themselves face. It is not easy to be an early adopter. We must support influencers in creating the change we want to see.

The "system"

You'd be forgiven by now for thinking I'm an eternal optimist. But remember: I have years of training as an auditor and senior finance leader. I view the world in a very analytical and critical way, and I am highly realistic. I'm under no illusions that changing the system will be easy.

The system includes people: partners in professional services firms, executives in corporations, managing directors in banks. It includes policies: policies that are archaic and non-inclusive; policies that are not enacted, enforced, or encouraged. It includes structures: hierarchy, bureaucracy, company politics and departments operating as silos . And it includes culture: presenteeism, social norms, valued skills. The system is big, and deeply entrenched.

So again, we need to come back to first principles here. Influence happens one person at a time. We need to gradually and respectfully challenge the status quo and those in executive leadership. I think we can all take the lead of RBA Governor Philip Lowe's daughter, who was told in high school[23], 'If you have a mother or father with influence, you should ask them what they're doing to help women.' If you have a professional relationship with someone in a position of influence, you absolutely should ask them what they're doing to help women in finance.

If attracting, developing, and retaining women in finance is a strategic imperative for your organisation, you need to heed the words in this book. You need to align people to purpose and include people of all genders at all levels within the organisation. You need to equip women with the skills and structures to bring their purpose into alignment with the organisation's purpose, and you need to empower them to feel confident in doing so.

Change is an iterative process

It is a journey, and one that you can accelerate if it's important to you. Don't leave it all up to the individual women of your organisation. Where your energy goes, the results will flow.

Results beyond the numbers.

AN INVITATION TO CONTINUE THE CONVERSATION

This book is about creating meaningful change so that women in finance like you can amplify your impact at work in a way that's congruent with your purpose. It's about the change you can actively contribute to through provoking the right conversations. It's only fitting, therefore, that I invite you to continue the conversation with me so that we can together create sustainable change for both you and women to come.

My regular blog posts are a great way to stay on track connected with both me and my latest insights and tools to help you on your journey. Help is also available in other forms. My executive coaching programs are a great option if you want personal and targeted support with a specific focus and outcome in mind. If you want to do the work with a group of like-minded women, you are also welcome to join one of my women in finance training programs.

If you have a network of women in finance within your organisation who need nurturing, guidance and support, I also run my women in finance leadership programs in-house, which consider all three elements of the organisational ecosystem. I also regularly speak, consult and mentor within organisations on how to amplify and leverage performance through strategic leadership and team cohesion.

If you simply want connect and share a love of good wine and food, you might like to check out my Leading Women in Finance Networking Group: Connections Beyond the Numbers.

By reading this book, you have ignited the energy within yourself to take the next step in your finance career. It is now up to you to grasp the opportunities you have available with the impetus to thrive.

Results beyond the numbers is about creating results that are meaningful to you. I'd love to know what 'results beyond the numbers' means to you.

Alena

alenabennett.com.au
/in/alenabennett/
@alenabennett
hello@alenabennett.com.au

NOTES AND REFERENCES

1. Egon Zehnder Diversity Council, "2018 Global Board Diversity Tracker: Female CEOs and CFOs in Global, 2018", Egon Zehnder, December 2018, https://www.egonzehnder.com/global-board-diversity-tracker/customize-the-data?report=Female+CEOs+and+CFOs&subgroup=Global&year=2018

2. Peters, Sandy and Kleszczewski, Catherine, "New Public Company Auditor Disclosures: Who Audits the Company You Invest In? How Long Have They Been The Auditor?", CFA Institute, 2018, https://www.cfainstitute.org/-/media/documents/article/position-paper/new-public-company-auditor-disclosures.ashx

3. Wooton, Hannah, "Where are all the women?", Money Management, 2018, https://www.moneymanagement.com.au/features/where-are-all-women

4. Chief Executive Women, "ASX200 Senior Executive Consensus 2019", Chief Executive Women, 2019, https://cew.org.au/wp-content/uploads/2019/09/190905-Census-FINAL.pdf

5. Chin, Stacey, Krivkovich, Alexis and Nadeau, Marie-Claude, "Closing the Gap: Leadership perspectives on promoting women in financial services", McKinsey & Company, 2018, https://www.mckinsey.com/industries/financial-services/our-insights/closing-the-gap-leadership-perspectives-on-promoting-women-in-financial-services

6. Hunt, Vivian, Prince, Sara, Dixon-Fyle, Sundiatu and Yee, Lareina, "Delivering through Diversity", McKinsey & Company, January 2018, https://www.mckinsey.com/~/media/mckinsey/business%20functions/organization/our%20insights/delivering%20through%20diversity/delivering-through-diversity_full-report.ashx

7. Rock, David and Cox, Christine, "SCARF® in 2012: Updating the social neuroscience of collaborating with others", NeuroLeadership Journal, Issue 4 October 2012

8. Pink, Daniel, Drive, Cannongate Books, 2011

9   Sinek, Simon, Start With Why: How great leaders inspire everyone to take action, The Penguin Group, 2009

10 Goldsmith, Marshall, What Got You Here Won't Get You There: How successful people become even more successful, Profile Books Ltd, 2012

11 Covey, Stephen R., The 7 Habits of Highly Effective People: Powerful Lessons in Personal Change, Simon & Schuster UK Ltd, 2004

12 Barberio, Joseph, "This Comic Perfectly Explains the Mental Load Working Mothers Bear", Working Mother, Updated November 2018, https://www.workingmother.com/this-comic-perfectly-explains-mental-load-working-mothers-bear

13 Lieberman, Matthew D., Rock, David, Grant Halvorson, Heidi, Cox, Christine, "Breaking Bias Updated: The SEEDS® model", NeuroLeadership Journal, Volume 6 November 2015

14 Chamorro-Premuzic, Tomas, Why Do So Many Incompetent Men Become Leaders? (and how to fix it), Harvard Business Review Press, 2019

15 Tarbox, Katherine, "Is #MeToo Backlash Hurting Women's Opportunities in Finance?", HBR.org, March 2018, https://hbr.org/2018/03/is-metoo-backlash-hurting-womens-opportunities-in-finance

16 Bregman, Peter, 18 Minutes: Find your Focus, Master Distraction, and Get the Right Things Done, Orion Books Ltd, 2012

17 Gollwitzer, Peter, "Implementation Intentions: Strong Effects of Simple Plans", The American Psychologist, 1999, https://pdfs.semanticscholar.org/4c21/6c0ceeef2e2745d113c77a417133c2084dd9.pdf

18 Deane, Sarah, "The Power of Data for Meaningful Conversations", Huffpost, October 2017, https://www.huffpost.com/entry/the-power-of-data-for-meaningful-conversations_b_5a05d425e4b0ee8ec36940e6

19 Detert, James R., "Cultivating Everyday Courage: The right way to speak truth to power", HBR November-December 2019, https://hbr.org/2018/11/cultivating-everyday-courage

20 Pink, Daniel, When: The Scientific Secrets of Perfect Timing, 2018, Audiobook on Audible.com

21 Cihak, Martin and Sahay, Ratna, "Women in Finance: An Economic Case for Gender Equality", IMFBlog, September 2018, https://blogs.imf.org/2018/09/19/women-in-finance-an-economic-case-for-gender-equality/

22 United Nations, "UN adopts new Global Goals charting sustainable development for people and planet by 2030", UN News, September 2015, https://news.un.org/en/story/2015/09/509732-un-adopts-new-global-goals-charting-sustainable-development-people-and-planet

23 Hartcher, Peter, "What's going wrong with Australia, RBA Chief Philip Lowe fears the economy's time is up", Good Weekend, September 2019, https://www.smh.com.au/business/banking-and-finance/what-s-going-wrong-with-australia-rba-chief-philip-lowe-fears-the-economy-s-time-is-up-20190903-p52nbu.html

www.ingramcontent.com/pod-product-compliance
Lightning Source LLC
Chambersburg PA
CBHW071345080526
44587CB00017B/2971